JN448090

다양한 컴퓨터 기능을 이용한

전산물리

Computational Physics using Various Aspects of Computer

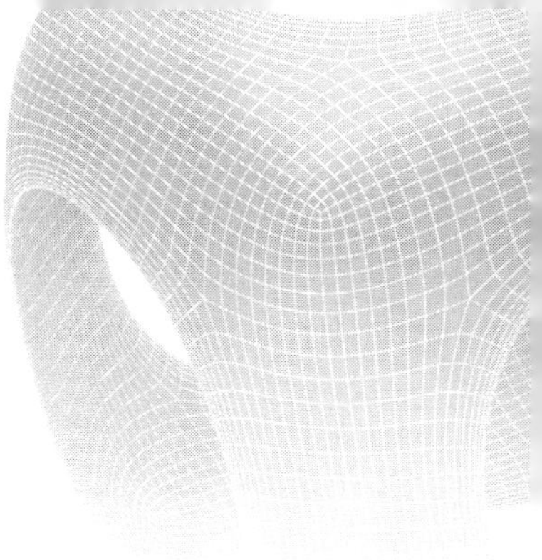

Suk-Joon Lee

이 석 준 저

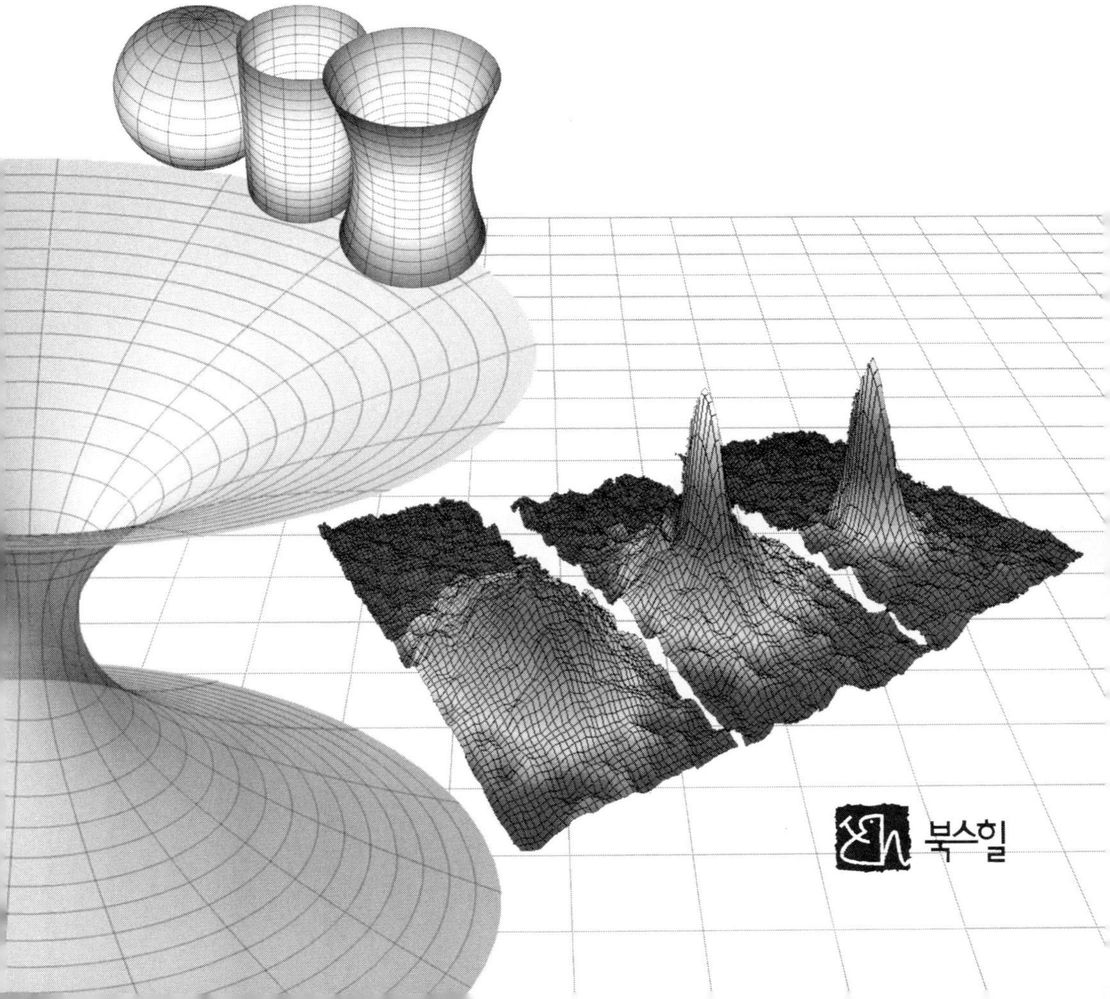

북스힐

Computational Physics using Various Aspects of Computer
(다양한 컴퓨터 기능을 이용한 전산물리)
Suk-Joon Lee (이석준)

Copyright ⓒ 2013 Books Hill & Ichi Science
ISBN-13:9788955265521
17, Hancheon-ro 153-gil,
Gangbuk-gu, Seoul, Korea
Tel : (82) 2 994 0071
Fax: (82) 2 994 0073

Preface

This book is a compilation with some extension of my lecture notes on computational physics (http://comphys.khu.ac.kr) which have been taught for many years as an undergraduate course. In the past, computer had been used in physics mostly to study complex physical system numerically. Since computers in the world are connected each other through worldwide network now, physicists use computer not only for numerical study of complex system but also for controlling experiment, analysing data, exchanging information, etc. Thus in this book, various usages of computer and internet in physics are also briefly discussed beside the various numerical methods.

To familiarize the methods discussed in this book, it is best to practice them by applying to actual problem. To aid this, basic commands in Unix/Linux operating system, the structure and basic commands of hyper text markup language (HTML) for web page, and basic commands of Fortran and C languages for numerical analysis of physical phenomena are included in Appendix. Many journals accept manuscript file written in LaTeX for publication of research papers. The structure and commands of LaTeX are also included in Appendix. This book is also edited using LaTeX.

Even though various aspects of computers in physics are discussed briefly, I believe this book would be very helpful for students in their study or research in physics.

2013.12.

S. J. Lee

머리말

물리를 전공하는 학부 학생들을 위하여 수 년간 강의하였던 강의록을 (http://comphys.khu.ac.kr) 보강해서 정리하였다. 과거에는 복잡한 물리 관계식을 수치적으로 계산하는 목적으로만 computer를 사용하였으나 전 세계의 computer가 network으로 서로 연결되어 있는 현재에는 수치계산 이외에도 실험 관리, 실험자료 분석, 정보 교환 등 여러 목적으로 computer를 사용하고 있다. 따라서 수치계산법 외에도 물리학 연구과정에서 computer를 사용하는 여러 경우들과 물리학이 computer와 network 개발에 기여하는 내용들까지 개략적이지만 본 전산물리에 정리하였다.

여기서 다룬 내용들을 제대로 습득하기 위해서는 computer를 이용하여 실제로 적용·응용해 보아야 한다. 이에 도움이 되도록 Unix/Linux Operating System에서의 명령어 (command)와, web page 작성을 위한 Hyper Text Markup Language (HTML), 수치계산을 위한 Fortran과 C Language의 기본 구조와 이들의 주요 command들을 부록에 간략하게 첨부하였다. 또한 연구결과를 학술지에 게제하고자 할 때 전 세계의 주요 학술지들이 받아들이고 있는 문서 편집기이고 본 전산물리를 편집하기 위하여 사용한 LaTeX의 구조와 여러 command 및 예문을 부록에 첨부하였다.

기본적인 개념들만 대략적으로 정리하였으나 물리를 공부하거나 연구를 수행하는 데 많은 도움이 되길 바라는 바이다.

2013.12.

이 석준

Contents

1 Computer and Internet 1

1.1 Physics and Computer 1

1.1.1 Computer in Physics 1

1.1.2 Physics for Computer Development 1

1.2 Internet and Physics 2

1.2.1 Internet in Physics 2

1.2.2 Network Components 2

1.2.3 Computers and OS (Operating System) 2

1.2.4 Connection 3

1.2.5 Connection Purpose 3

1.3 Computer Programming 5

1.3.1 Programming 5

1.3.2 Fortran Language 5

1.3.3 C Language 6

2 Basic Mathematical Operations 7

2.1 Lagrange n-points Interpolation 7

2.2 Numerical Differentiation 8

2.3 Higher Order Differentiation 9
2.4 Numerical Integral 10
2.5 Finding Roots; Finding Zero Points 11

3 First Order Ordinary Differential Equation 13
3.1 Euler's Method 14
3.2 Using Extrapolation 14
3.3 Using Interpolation 15
3.4 Runge-Kutta Methods 15
3.5 Stability 16

4 Boundary Value and Eigenvalue Problems 17
4.1 Numerov Algorithm 18
4.2 Green Function Solution; Boundary Condition 19
4.3 Eigenvalue Problem 21

5 Special Functions and Gaussian Quadrature 23
5.1 Special Functions and Recurrence Relations 23
5.2 Gaussian Quadrature; Integral using Special Function 27

6 Matrix Analysis 29
6.1 Matrix Inversion 30
6.2 Eigenvalue Problem 32
6.3 Inverse Vector Iteration 33
6.4 Damped Gradient Iteration 34
6.5 Lanczos Algorithm 34

7 Discretized Grid Space in Higher Dimension 37

7.1 Discretization and Variational Principle 38

7.2 Boundary Value Problem 39

7.3 Iterative Gauss-Seidel Method 40

7.4 Gaussian Elimination 41

8 Monte-Carlo Simulation 45

8.1 Monte-Carlo Method 45

8.2 Metropolis Algorithm 47

9 Computer and Experiment 49

9.1 Computer in Experiment 49

9.2 Connection of Computer and Experimental Equipment 49

10 Data Analysis 55

10.1 Mean Value and Standard Deviation 55

10.2 Chi-Square Fitting and Error Analysis 58

10.3 Fast Fourier Transform (FFT) 62

10.4 Wavelet Analysis 64

11 Text Editing and Graphics for Reports 65

11.1 Graphics 65

11.2 Text Editing Program 65

11.3 Presentation 66

A Unix Commands 67

B HTML Commands **71**

C Fortran Commands **77**

D C Commands **83**

E LaTeX **89**

E.1 Basic Structure of LaTeX File 89

E.2 LaTeX Commands 91

E.3 Sample LaTeX 104

Chapter 1

Computer and Internet

1.1 Physics and Computer

1.1.1 Computer in Physics

- Numerical calculation, simulation : complex nonlinear system
- Symbolic Math Equation Manipulation : Mathematica, Maple
- Controlling experiment, data analysis : LabView, MatLab
- Writing paper, drawing figures : Word processor, Graphics
- Information and data exchange : Network ; www, email, ftp ...
- Virtual demonstration : Java, Flash

1.1.2 Physics for Computer Development

- CPU(Central Processing Unit), GPU(Graphic Processing Unit), PPU(Physics Processing Unit), Math processor
- IC Chip, Semiconducting material
- Memory elements : magnetic, optical, atomic ...
- Peripherals : printer, scanner, OCR ...
- Display : VCR, (TFT) LCD, FED, Plasma, LED, OLED ...

- Communication media : cable (phone, TV, power), optical fiber, wireless (wave) ...

1.2 Internet and Physics

1.2.1 Internet in Physics

- Preprint depository : Example; http://xxx.lanl.gov/
- Data exchange : email, ftp, remote login,
- Calculation through PC network, Grid Computing :
  Example ; http://www.koreaathome.org/
- Paper submission to Journal :
  Example ; http://jkps.kps.or.kr/home/journal/article/submission/
- Published journal access :
  Example ; http://www.kps.or.kr/home/kor/journal/JKPS/

1.2.2 Network Components

- Network cable : Ethernet, Phone line, Cable TV line, Power line, Optical fiber, Wave, Satellite, Token ring, FDDI
- Network Interface Board : Modem, LAN card, USB, WiFi, BlueTooth
- Communication control protocol : TCP/IP, SLIP/PPP, Winsock
- Communication Service Protocol : Telnet, Xterm, SSH, FTP, Mail, http

1.2.3 Computers and OS (Operating System)

- Personal Computers : DOS, Windows, NT, XP, Linux, Mackintosh
- Work Station (WS) : Unix (see Appendix A), VMS
- Main frame, Super computer, Cluster Computing
- CPU(Central Processing Unit), GPU(Graphic Processing Unit), PPU(Physics Processing Unit), Math processor

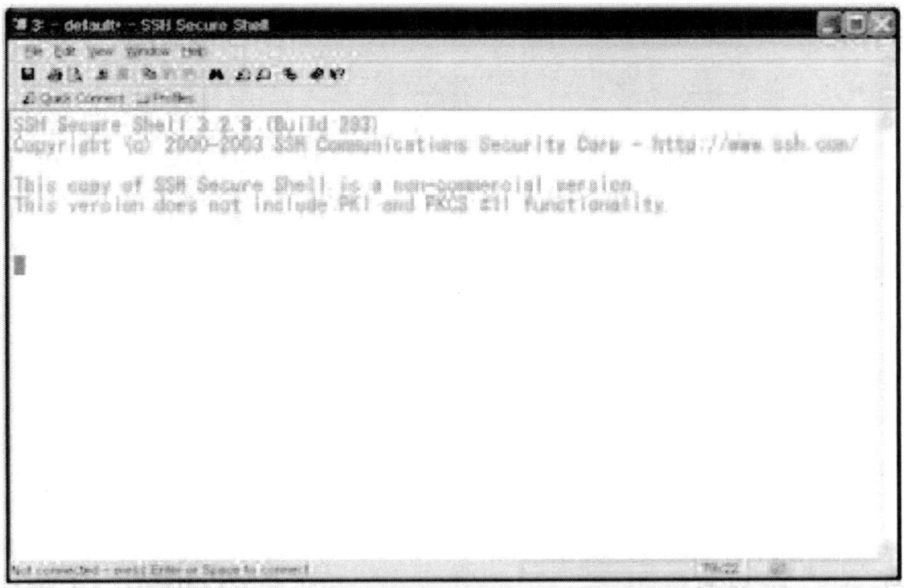

Figure 1.1: SSH Secure Shell Client

1.2.4 Connection

- Terminal : WS or main system with terminal server ; one to many
- Virtual terminal : Terminal emulator ; PC to WS ; many to many
- Xterminal : X-Window ; PC to WS
- Modem : Dialup, DSL, Cable, WiFi, WiBro
- LAN : IP address, Domain Name

1.2.5 Connection Purpose

- Remote login : Telnet, Rlogin, Host ; NetTerm, X-Win, VTE, htn, Dialup, PuTTY, SSH ...

  Telnet command
  telnet comphys.khu.ac.kr
  Login procedure (username, password)

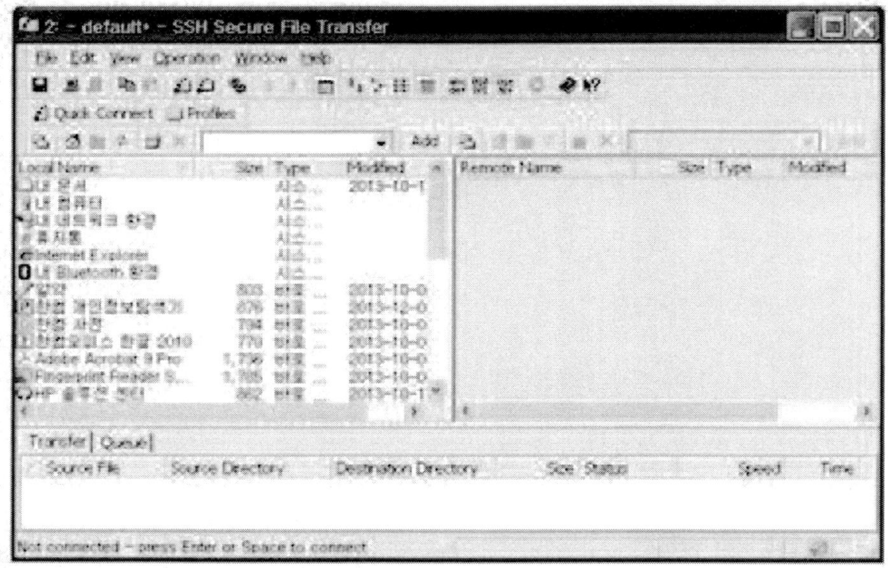

Figure 1.2: SSH Secure File Transfer

System Commands

Dialup Modem

atdt 205-xxxx (961-xxxx∼xxxy)

at khnet# connect comphys

Login procedure (username, password)

- E-mail : mail, elm, mailx, pine, eudora, outlook express, web mail ...
- File exchange : FTP, WS_FTP, WinSCP, PSFTP, SSHftp, Kermit, X-modem, Z-modem ...

FTP command

ftp comphys.kyunghee.ac.kr

login procedure (username, password)

Commands ; help, dir, put, mput, get, mget, cd, bin, ascii ...

- Information exchange : World Wide Web (http), News ...

WWW viewer : Netscape, Internet explore, Mosaic, Gopher,

Mozilla, Firefox ...
Web language : HTML (hyper text markup language, Appendix B),
CGI, Java Script ...

1.3 Computer Programming

1.3.1 Programming

1. Analyze Problem (structure, relation, equation ...)
2. Draw Flow Chart
3. Program
4. Compile and Link
5. Execute (Run) Program
6. Input Data → Program → Output Results
7. Analyze Results

* See Appendix A for Unix/Linux commands.

1.3.2 Fortran Language

- fort77 -o filexec -l library filename.f : Compile and Link Fortran Program "filename.f" and create a file "filexec" at Unix System (or f77)
- ./filexec : Execute the execution file created by fort77 at Unix system
- Structure of Fortran Program

```
PROGRAM progname [(......)]
.........
.........
STOP
END
SUBROUTINE subname (......)
.........
```

```
.........
RETURN
END
type FUNCTION funcname (......)
.........
.........
RETURN
END
```

- See Appendix C for commands.

1.3.3 C Language

- cc -o filexec filename.c : Compile and Link C Program "filename.c" and create an execution file "filexec" at Unix System (or g77)
- ./filexec : execute the execution file created by cc at Unix system
- Structure of C Program

```
Preprocessor (#include, #define .....)
main ()
{......... ;
.......... ;
.......... ;}
type subname (.....)
{......... ;
.......... ;
.......... ;}
```

- See Appendix D for commands.

Chapter 2

Basic Mathematical Operations

2.1 Lagrange n-points Interpolation

For n-points, Lagrange interpolation (내삽법) of function $f(x)$ is

$$f(x) = \sum_{i=1}^{n} \prod_{j \neq i}^{n} \left(\frac{x - x_j}{x_i - x_j} \right) f_i \tag{2.1}$$

where f_i is the value of function $f(x_i)$ at grid point x_i. For 2-points, as a special case,

$$f(x) \approx \frac{x - x_1}{x_0 - x_1} f_0 + \frac{x - x_0}{x_1 - x_0} f_1 = f_0 + \frac{f_1 - f_0}{x_1 - x_0}(x - x_0). \tag{2.2}$$

If we have equally spaced grid points $x_i = ih$ with step size h, the interpolation around $x_0 = 0$ is

$$f(x) = f_0 \pm \frac{f_{\pm 1} - f_0}{h} x \tag{2.3}$$

for 2-points. For 3-points

$$f(x) \approx f_0 + \frac{f_1 - f_{-1}}{2h} x + \frac{f_1 - 2f_0 + f_{-1}}{2h^2} x^2. \tag{2.4}$$

For 4-points

$$\begin{aligned} f(x) &\approx f_0 \pm \frac{1}{6h}(-2f_{\mp 1} - 3f_0 + 6f_{\pm 1} - f_{\pm 2})x + \frac{1}{2h^2}(f_{-1} - 2f_0 + f_1)x^2 \\ &\pm \frac{1}{6h^3}(-f_{\mp 1} + 3f_0 - 3f_{\pm 1} + f_{\pm 2})x^3. \end{aligned} \tag{2.5}$$

For 5 points

$$\begin{aligned} f(x) &= f_0 + \frac{1}{12h}(f_{-2} - 8f_{-1} + 8f_1 - f_2)x \\ &+ \frac{1}{24h^2}(-f_{-2} + 16f_{-1} - 30f_0 + 16f_1 - f_2)x^2 \\ &+ \frac{1}{12h^3}(-f_{-2} + 2f_{-1} - 2f_1 + f_2)x^3 \\ &+ \frac{1}{24h^4}(f_{-2} - 4f_{-1} + 6f_0 - 4f_1 + f_2)x^4. \end{aligned} \tag{2.6}$$

2.2 Numerical Differentiation

Taylor series expansion;

$$f(x) = f_0 + xf' + \frac{x^2}{2!}f'' + \frac{x^3}{3!}f''' + \frac{x^4}{4!}f'''' + \cdots. \tag{2.7}$$

At the discretized grid points,

$$\begin{aligned} f(0) &= f_0, \\ f(\pm h) &= f_{\pm 1} = f_0 \pm hf' + \frac{h^2}{2!}f'' \pm \frac{h^3}{3!}f''' + \frac{h^4}{4!}f'''' + \cdots, \\ f(\pm 2h) &= f_{\pm 2} = f_0 \pm 2hf' + \frac{4h^2}{2!}f'' \pm \frac{8h^3}{3!}f''' + \frac{16h^4}{4!}f'''' + \cdots. \end{aligned} \tag{2.8}$$

Using Eqs.(2.8) or by differentiating the interpolated function of Sect.2.1 we can obtain the numerical differential form of a function.

First order numerical differential form of function $f(x)$ at $x = 0$:
For 2-points (linear);

$$f' \approx \frac{f_1 - f_0}{h} + O(h) = \frac{f_0 - f_{-1}}{h} + O(h). \tag{2.9}$$

For 3-points, from Eq.(2.4) or Eqs.(2.8);

$$\begin{aligned} f_1 - f_{-1} &= 2hf' + \frac{h^3}{3}f''' + O(h^5), \\ f' &= \frac{f_1 - f_{-1}}{2h} - \frac{h^2}{6}f''' + O(h^4) \approx \frac{f_1 - f_{-1}}{2h} + O(h^2). \end{aligned} \quad (2.10)$$

This 3-point differential looks like 2-point differential with step size $2h$. However 3-point differential form is symmetric around $x = 0$ where we evaluate the differential while 2-point differential form is not. For 4-points;

$$f' = \pm \frac{1}{6h}(-2f_{\mp 1} - 3f_0 + 6f_{\pm 1} - f_{\pm 2}) + O(h^3). \quad (2.11)$$

For 5-points;

$$f' \approx \frac{1}{12h}[f_{-2} - 8f_{-1} + 8f_1 - f_2] + O(h^4). \quad (2.12)$$

2.3 Higher Order Differentiation

No 2-points 2nd order differential.
3-points 2nd order differential, from Eqs.(2.8),

$$\begin{aligned} f_1 - 2f_0 + f_{-1} &= h^2 f'' + O(h^4), \\ f'' &= \frac{f_1 - 2f_0 + f_{-1}}{h^2} + O(h^2). \end{aligned} \quad (2.13)$$

4-points 2nd order differential

$$f\,'' = \frac{1}{h^2}(f_{-1} - 2f_0 + f_1) + O(h^3). \quad (2.14)$$

5-points 2nd order differential

$$f'' = \frac{1}{12h^2}(-f_{-2} + 16f_{-1} - 30f_0 + 16f_1 - f_2) + O(h^4). \quad (2.15)$$

No 3-points 3rd order differential.
4-points 3rd order differential

$$f''' \approx \pm \frac{1}{h^3}(-f_{\mp 1} + 3f_0 - 3f_{\pm 1} + f_{\pm 2}). \quad (2.16)$$

5-points 3rd order differential

$$f''' \approx \frac{1}{2h^3}(-f_{-2} + 2f_{-1} - 2f_1 + f_2). \tag{2.17}$$

No 4-points 4th order differential.
5-points 4th order differential

$$f^{(iv)} \approx \frac{1}{h^4}(f_{-2} - 4f_{-1} + 6f_0 - 4f_1 + f_2). \tag{2.18}$$

2.4 Numerical Integral

We can obtain numerical integration form of function $f(x)$ using the interpolation given in Sect.2.1.

Trapezoidal rule : 2-points linear integral
Two trapezoidal integrals for 3-points,

$$\int_{-h}^{h} f(x)dx = \frac{h}{2}(f_{-1} + 2f_0 + f_1) + O(h^3). \tag{2.19}$$

Simpson's rule : 3-points integral (cf. 3-points Lagrange Interpolation)

$$\int_{-h}^{h} f(x)dx = \frac{h}{3}(f_{-1} + 4f_0 + f_1) + O(h^5). \tag{2.20}$$

For $a < x < b$, by Simpson's rule,

$$\int_{a}^{b} f(x)dx = \frac{h}{3}[f(a) + 4f(a+h) + 2f(a+2h) + 4f(a+3h) + 2f(a+4h) + \cdots + 2f(b-2h) + 4f(b-h) + f(b)] \tag{2.21}$$

by discretizing into even number of equal segments (grid size) h.

4-points integral : Simpson's 3/8 rule

$$\int_{0}^{3h} f(x)dx = \frac{3h}{8}(f_0 + 3f_1 + 3f_2 + f_3) + O(h^5). \tag{2.22}$$

5-points integral : Bode's rule

$$\int_{0}^{5h} f(x)dx = \frac{2h}{45}(7f_0 + 32f_1 + 12f_2 + 32f_3 + 7f_4) + O(h^7). \tag{2.23}$$

Note here that the 3-point integral and the 4-point integral have the same order of error $O(h^5)$ due to the $\pm$ sign of the odd terms in Eq.(2.8). Thus we usually use 3-point Simpson or 5-point Bode's rule which have the midpoint of integral range as one of the grid points.

If function $f(x)$ has both fast varying region and slowly varying region then we can use different grid size for different region. If we can change fast varying function such as $g(x)e^{-x}$ or function with singular points such as $(1-x^2)^{-1/2}$ with singular point $x = \pm 1$ to a smoothly varying function without singular point within the integration region by changing variable then we can use equal grid size with the new variable after changing the function as a function of the new variable.

2.5 Finding Roots; Finding Zero Points

Simple method using half step size. Choose two points x_i and $x_{i+1} = x_i + h$. If

$$f(x_{i+1})f(x_i) > 0, \tag{2.24}$$

then move to next point. If $|f(x_i)| < |f(x_{i+1})|$ then change h to $-h$. If

$$f(x_{i+1})f(x_i) < 0, \tag{2.25}$$

then change h to $h/2$. If this condition is satisfied with $|x_{i+1} - x_i|$ less than allowed error then the zero point is x_i.

Newton-Raphson method. Find the new point x_{i+1} using the differential $f'(x)$ of function $f(x)$.

$$\begin{aligned} f(x_{i+1}) &\approx f(x_i) + (x_{i+1} - x_i)f'(x_i) = 0, \\ x_{i+1} &= x_i - \frac{f(x_i)}{f'(x_i)}. \end{aligned} \tag{2.26}$$

Secant method. Use $f(x_{i-1})$ and $f(x_i)$ for $f'(x_i)$ in Newton-Raphson method.

$$\begin{aligned} f'(x_i) &\approx \frac{f(x_i) - f(x_{i-1})}{x_i - x_{i-1}}, \\ x_{i+1} &= x_i - f(x_i)\frac{x_i - x_{i-1}}{f(x_i) - f(x_{i-1})}. \end{aligned} \tag{2.27}$$

Chapter 3

First Order Ordinary Differential Equation

Solve first order ordinary differential equation

$$\frac{dy(x)}{dx} = f(x, y) \tag{3.1}$$

for function $y(x)$ with initial condition $y(x_0) = y_0$. This can be solved by recursion relation starting from y_0 at x_0.

Hamilton's equation of motion;

$$\begin{aligned} \frac{dq}{dt} &= \frac{\partial H(q,p,t)}{\partial q}, \\ \frac{dp}{dt} &= -\frac{\partial H(q,p,t)}{\partial q}. \end{aligned}$$

A second order differential equation can be replaced by two coupled first order differential equations. Newton's equation of motion;

$$\begin{aligned} m\frac{d^2x}{dt^2} &= f(t,x,v), \\ \frac{dx}{dt} &= v, \\ \frac{dv}{dt} &= f(t,x,v)/m. \end{aligned}$$

3.1 Euler's Method

Using two point differential form, the recursion relation of Euler's method is

$$y_{n+1} = y_n + hf(x_n, y_n) + O(h^2). \tag{3.2}$$

Since $y' = f(x, y(x))$, we have

$$y'' = \frac{d}{dx}f(x,y) = \frac{\partial f}{\partial x} + \frac{\partial f}{\partial y}f. \tag{3.3}$$

Thus from Taylor expansion

$$y_{n+1} = y_n + hy'_n + \frac{h^2}{2}y''_n + \frac{h^3}{3!}y'''_n + \cdots, \tag{3.4}$$

we can get higher order recursion relation

$$y_{n+1} = y_n + hf_n + \frac{h^2}{2}\left[\frac{\partial f}{\partial x} + f\frac{\partial f}{\partial y}\right]_n + O(h^3). \tag{3.5}$$

3.2 Using Extrapolation

Implicit methods using integral of f,

$$y_{n+1} = y_n + \int_{x_n}^{x_{n+1}} f(x,y)dx. \tag{3.6}$$

Use extrapolation (외삽법) or interpolation (내삽법) for $f(x, y)$ here.

Extrapolating $f(x, y)$ using two points of x_n and x_{n-1} and then integrating $f(x, y)$ for $x_n \leq x \leq x_{n+1}$, we get Adams-Bashforth 2-step Method

$$y_{n+1} = y_n + \frac{h}{2}(3f_n - f_{n-1}) + O(h^3). \tag{3.7}$$

Extension to multi-step method using multi-points extrapolation such as three points (x_n, x_{n-1}, x_{n-2}) quadratic extrapolation or four points (x_n, x_{n-1}, x_{n-2}, x_{n-3}) cubic extrapolation and then integrating $f(x, y)$ for $x_n \leq x \leq x_{n+1}$:

$$y_{n+1} = y_n + \frac{h}{24}(55f_n - 59f_{n-1} + 37f_{n-2} - 9f_{n-3}) + O(h^4) \tag{3.8}$$

for 4-step method.

3.3 Using Interpolation

Adams-Moulton Method: Use interpolation of $f(x, y)$ including x_n and x_{n+1} points. Using three points of x_{n-1}, x_n, and x_{n+1}, the Adams-Moulton 2-step method is

$$y_{n+1} = \frac{h}{12}(5f_{n+1} + 8f_n - f_{n-1}) + O(h^4). \tag{3.9}$$

Using four points of x_{n-2}, x_{n-1}, x_n, and x_{n+1} it becomes 3-step method:

$$y_{n+1} = \frac{h}{24}(9f_{n+1} + 19f_n - 5f_{n-1} + f_{n-2}) + O(h^5). \tag{3.10}$$

The unknown value of y_{n+1} is involved in Adams-Moulton method through $f_{n+1} = f(x_{n+1}, y_{n+1})$. For this problem use Predictor-Corrector Algorithm. That is, first, predict the values of y_n at point x_n for every points of $n = 1$, 2, 3, $\cdots$, N then use these values in the right hand side of Eq.(3.9) to obtain corrected new value of y_{n+1} for every point. Usually use the corrected values for y_1, y_2, $\cdots$, y_n together with the predicted value of y_{n+1} to evaluate the corrected new value of y_{n+1}. Repeat this process until the value of y_n approaches to the value of y_n at previous stage within allowed error.

3.4 Runge-Kutta Methods

Use three points Simpson rule for the integral of $f(x, y)$ from y_n to y_{n+1} with three points interpolation of x_n, $x_{n+1/2}$, and x_{n+1}.

$$\begin{aligned} y_{n+1} &= y_n + \int_{y_n}^{y_{n+1}} f(x, y)dx \\ &\approx y_n + \frac{h}{6}\Big[f(x_n, y_n) + 4f(x_{n+1/2}, y_{n+1/2}) + f(x_{n+1}, y_{n+1})\Big] + O(h^5) \end{aligned} \tag{3.11}$$

This equation involves unknown values of $y_{n+1/2}$ and y_{n+1}. Depending on how these values are approximated, this method becomes third order or fourth order Runge-Kutta Method.

Three point third order Runge-Kutta method;

$$\begin{aligned} k_1 &= hf(x_n, y_n), \\ k_2 &= hf(x_n + \frac{1}{2}h, y_n + \frac{1}{2}k_1), \end{aligned}$$

$$\begin{aligned} k_3 &= hf(x_n + h, y_n - k_1 + 2k_2), \\ y_{n+1} &= y_n + \frac{1}{6}(k_1 + 4k_2 + k_3) + O(h^4). \end{aligned} \tag{3.12}$$

Three point fourth order Runge-Kutta method;

$$\begin{aligned} k_1 &= hf(x_n, y_n), \\ k_2 &= hf(x_n + \frac{1}{2}h, y_n + \frac{1}{2}k_1), \\ k_3 &= hf(x_n + \frac{1}{2}h, y_n + \frac{1}{2}k_2), \\ k_4 &= hf(x_n + h, y_n + k_3), \\ y_{n+1} &= y_n + \frac{1}{6}(k_1 + 2k_2 + 2k_3 + k4) + O(h^5). \end{aligned} \tag{3.13}$$

3.5 Stability

Since the error accumulates as integrate through from initial point to final point using the recurrence relation, the direction of integration may be vital for some function of $f(x, y)$. For example, $\frac{dy}{dx} = f(x, y) = -y$ has the solution $y(x) = e^{-x}$ which becomes smaller and smaller fast as x becomes larger. If we integrate out starting from $x = 0$ with $y(0) = 1$, then the accumulated error could be larger than the value of y_N at large x_N. If we integrate in from x_N with y_N, then the accumulated error could be much smaller than y_1 at small x_1.

Chapter 4

Boundary Value and Eigenvalue Problems

Solve second order linear differential equation

$$\frac{d^2y(x)}{dx^2} + k^2(x)y(x) = S(x) \tag{4.1}$$

for function $y(x)$. When the source term $S(x)$ is not zero, this inhomogeneous linear differential equation can be treated as a boundary value problem with boundary condition (경계조건) of $y(x_0) = y_0$ and $y(x_N) = y_N$ or as an initial value problem with intitial condition (초기조건) of $y(x_0) = y_0$ and $y'(x_0) = y'_0$ or equivalently $y(x_0) = y_0$ and $y(x_1) = y_1$. If the source term is zero then this becomes eigenvalue problem (고유값 문제) with boundary condition.

Wave equation for normal mode in 1-d;

$$\frac{d^2\psi(x)}{d^2x} = -k^2(x)\psi(x). \tag{4.2}$$

Poisson equation for electric potential;

$$\nabla^2\phi(\vec{r}) \;\; = \;\; -\frac{1}{\epsilon_0}\rho(\vec{r}). \tag{4.3}$$

Time independent Schrödinger equation;

$$\left[-\frac{\hbar^2}{2m}\nabla^2 + V(\vec{r})\right]\psi(\vec{r}) \;\; = \;\; E\psi(\vec{r}). \tag{4.4}$$

In Cartesian 1-d, $\nabla^2 = \frac{d^2}{dx^2}$. In spherical coordinate system,

$$\begin{aligned}\nabla^2 &= \frac{1}{r^2}\frac{\partial}{\partial r}\left(r^2\frac{\partial}{\partial r}\right) + \frac{1}{r^2\sin\theta}\frac{\partial}{\partial\theta}\left(\sin\theta\frac{\partial}{\partial\theta}\right) + \frac{1}{r^2\sin^2\theta}\frac{\partial^2}{\partial\varphi^2} \\ &= \frac{1}{r}\frac{\partial^2}{\partial r^2}r + \frac{1}{r^2}\frac{L^2}{\hbar^2}. \end{aligned} \tag{4.5}$$

For spherically symmetric system, i.e., for $\rho(\vec{r}) = \rho(r)$ or $V(\vec{r}) = V(r)$, the variables r, θ, and φ are separable

$$\psi(r,\theta,\varphi) = \frac{R(r)}{r}Y_{lm}(\theta,\varphi) \tag{4.6}$$

with spherical harmonic Y_{lm}. Then the equation for radial function R becomes

$$\frac{d^2R(r)}{dr^2} + \frac{2m}{\hbar^2}\left[E - V(r) - \frac{l(l+1)\hbar^2}{2mr^2}\right]R(r) = -\frac{1}{\epsilon_0}r\rho(r) \tag{4.7}$$

where the source term $\rho(r) = 0$ for the time independent Schrödinger equation and $E = 0$ and $V(r) = 0$ for the Poisson equation.

4.1 Numerov Algorithm

When the source $S(x)$ is not zero, the inhomogeneous linear differential equation Eq.(4.1) with boundary condition determines the response $y(x)$ to the source $S(x)$. From Eq.(2.8), for Eq.(4.1),

$$\begin{aligned} y_{n+1} - 2y_n + y_{n-1} &= h^2y_n'' + \frac{h^4}{12}y_n'''' + O(h^6) \\ &= h^2(S-k^2y)_n + \frac{h^4}{12}(S-k^2y)_n'' + O(h^6). \end{aligned} \tag{4.8}$$

Using Eq.(2.13) for $y'''' = (S-k^2y)''$,

$$\begin{aligned} \left(1+\frac{h^2}{12}k_{n+1}^2\right)y_{n+1} &- 2\left(1-5\frac{h^2}{12}k_n^2\right)y_n + \left(1+\frac{h^2}{12}k_{n-1}^2\right)y_{n-1} \\ &= \frac{h^2}{12}\left(S_{n+1}+10S_n+S_{n-1}\right) + O(h^6). \end{aligned} \tag{4.9}$$

This recursion relation can be used as an initial value problem. Starting from the two values of y_0 and y_1 or the two values y_N and y_{N-1}, evaluate values y_n at other points x_n recursively. The response $y(x)$ to the source $S(x)$ can also be found using Predictor-Corrector Algorithm for this recursion relation with boundary condition of $y(x_0) = y_0$ and $y(x_N) = y_N$ as discussed in Sect.3.3.

Since Eq.(4.1) is a linear differential equation, a large error at end points could occur even if we start with a small error at initial points. For an inhomogeneous linear differential equation the general solution is a sum of a particular solution of the inhomogeneous equation and a general solution of homogeneous differential equation. As a simple example,

$$\frac{d^2\phi(x)}{dx^2} = e^{-x} \tag{4.10}$$

has solution $\phi(x) = e^{-x}$ with boundary condition $\phi(0) = 1$. The homogeneous equation $d^2\phi(x)/dx^2 = 0$ has a general solution of $\phi(x) = a + bx$ with arbitrary constants a and b. Thus the general solution of Eq.(4.10), the linear differential equation with source term, is

$$\phi(x) = e^{-x} + a + bx. \tag{4.11}$$

Even if there is only a very small error in initial value y_0 and y_1, the error becomes larger and larger as $a + bx$ form in the recursive steps of Numerov method. However since we know the form of the error occurring due to the solution of homogeneous equation, we can compensate by hand after recursive calculation to remove this type of error. For the example of Eq.(4.10), subtract $a + bx$ from the values $\phi(x_n)$ obtained by the recurrence equation with the values of a and b determined to satisfy the boundary conditions. If we use predictor-corrector method with proper boundary condition then this problem does not occur. Another way of avoiding this kind of error is using Green function satisfying boundary condition at both side.

4.2 Green Function Solution; Boundary Condition

Gauss theorem;

$$\int_V \vec{\nabla} \cdot \vec{A} dV = \oint_S \vec{A} \cdot d\vec{S}. \tag{4.12}$$

Green's theorem, with $\vec{A} = \phi\nabla\psi$ and $\vec{B} = \psi\nabla\phi$,

$$\int_V \vec{\nabla}\cdot\left(\vec{A}-\vec{B}\right) dV = \int_V \left[\phi\nabla^2\psi - \psi\nabla^2\phi\right] dV = \oint_S \left[\phi\vec{\nabla}\psi - \psi\vec{\nabla}\phi\right]\cdot d\vec{S}.$$

For a linear differential equation,

$$\left[\nabla^2 + k^2(\vec{r})\right]\Psi(\vec{r}) = S(\vec{r}), \tag{4.13}$$

the corresponding Green function;

$$\left[\nabla^2 + k^2(\vec{r})\right] G(\vec{r},\vec{r}') = -4\pi\delta(\vec{r}-\vec{r}'). \tag{4.14}$$

Then

$$\begin{aligned}\Psi(\vec{r}) &= -\frac{1}{4\pi}\int G(\vec{r},\vec{r}')S(\vec{r}')dV \\ &\quad +\frac{1}{4\pi}\oint_S \left[G(\vec{r},\vec{r}')\vec{\nabla}'\Psi(\vec{r}') - \Psi(\vec{r}')\vec{\nabla}'G(\vec{r},\vec{r}')\right]\cdot d\vec{S}\end{aligned} \tag{4.15}$$

with Green's function satisfying a proper boundary condition.

In 1-d, the solution $\phi(x)$ of

$$\left[\frac{d^2}{dx^2} + k(x)\right]\phi(x) = S(x) \tag{4.16}$$

with boundary condition of $\phi(x=a)=0$ and $\phi(x=b)=0$ for $a \le x \le b$,

$$\phi(x) = \int_a^b G(x,x')S(x')dx', \tag{4.17}$$

where the Green's function $G(x,x')$ satisfies

$$\left[\frac{d^2}{dx^2} + k(x)\right] G(x,x') = \delta(x-x') \tag{4.18}$$

with proper boundary condition, i.e, $G(x,x') = 0$ when either of x or x' is at the bondary point a or b for this case. Integrating this

$$\left.\frac{dG}{dx}\right|_{x=x'+\epsilon} - \left.\frac{dG}{dx}\right|_{x=x'-\epsilon} = 1. \tag{4.19}$$

Using the homogeneous solution $\phi_<$ and $\phi_>$ of the linear differential equation without the source term with proper boundary condition at $x = a$ and

$x = b$, i.e., $\phi_<(x = a) = 0$ and $\phi_>(x = b) = 0$, the green function satisfying boundary condition of ϕ is

$$G(x, x') = \phi_<(x_<)\phi_>(x_>) \tag{4.20}$$

with $x_<$ and $x_>$ are the smaller one and larger one of x and x'. Thus

$$\phi(x) = \phi_>(x)\int_a^x \phi_<(x')S(x')dx' + \phi_<(x)\int_x^b \phi_>(x')S(x')dx'. \tag{4.21}$$

As an example, the radial equation of Poisson equation

$$\left[\frac{d^2}{dr^2} - \frac{l(l+1)}{r^2}\right]\phi(r) = S(r) \tag{4.22}$$

for $0 \leq r < \infty$ has

$$\phi_<(x) = r^{l+1} \quad ; \quad \phi_>(x) = -\frac{1}{2l+1}r^{-l}. \tag{4.23}$$

4.3 Eigenvalue Problem

Homogeneous linear differential equation without source term $S(x)$,

$$\left[\frac{d^2}{dx^2} + k^2(x)\right]\psi_n(x) = \lambda_n\psi_n(x) \tag{4.24}$$

in the range of $a \leq x \leq b$. The solution $\psi_n(x)$ can have an arbitrary overall scale thus have a normalization condition. Boundary condition at both end points $\psi(x_a) = \psi_a$ and $\psi(x_b) = \psi_b$ can be satisfied only for special values of λ_n. Such a value of λ_n is called eigenvalue and the corresponding $\psi_n(x)$ is the eigenfunction.

To solve eigenvalue problem use shooting method. Pick a trial value for λ_n (by estimating) and integrate from one end point with the corresponding boundary condition to the other end point and then check if it satisfies the boundary condition at that end point. Since $\psi_n(x)$ can have an arbitrary overall size, the numerical integral can be started with $\psi_n(a) = \psi_a$ and $\psi_n'(a) = \psi_a'$ with arbitrary value of ψ_a'. If it does not satisfy the boundary condition then do the same thing with a new trial value for λ_n. Repeat this process until the boundary condition is satisfied within allowed error. In choosing a new value of λ_n use the method of finding roots in Sect. 2.5.

If $\psi(x)$ goes to zero exponentially as approaching to the boundaries, then the error coming from the numerical integral can be too large to satisfy boundary condition. For such a case, integrate in from both end points with boundary condition and match smoothly the integrated wave function $\psi_<(x)$ and $\psi_>(x)$ at a matching point x_m where ψ is not too small.

$$\psi_<(x_m) = \psi_>(x_m) \quad ; \quad \frac{d\psi_<(x_m)}{dx} = \frac{d\psi_>(x_m)}{dx}. \tag{4.25}$$

Since the normalization condition, the matching condition can be reduced to

$$\frac{\psi_<(x_m - h)}{\psi_<(x_m)} - \frac{\psi_>(x_m - h)}{\psi_>(x_m)} = 0. \tag{4.26}$$

Chapter 5

Special Functions and Gaussian Quadrature

5.1 Special Functions and Recurrence Relations

Variables of Laplace equation $\nabla^2\Psi(\vec{r}) = 0$ in 3-dimension are separable, i.e.,

$$\begin{aligned}
\nabla^2\Psi(\vec{r}) &= \left[\frac{\partial^2}{\partial x^2} + \frac{\partial^2}{\partial y^2} + \frac{\partial^2}{\partial z^2}\right] X(x)Y(y)Z(z) \\
&= \left[\frac{1}{r}\frac{\partial^2}{\partial r^2}r + \frac{1}{r^2}\left(\frac{1}{\sin\theta}\frac{\partial}{\partial\theta}\sin\theta\frac{\partial}{\partial\theta} + \frac{1}{\sin^2\theta}\frac{\partial^2}{\partial\varphi^2}\right)\right]\frac{U(r)}{r}P(\theta)\Phi(\varphi) \\
&= \left[\frac{1}{\rho}\frac{\partial}{\partial\rho}\left(\rho\frac{\partial}{\partial\rho}\right) + \frac{1}{\rho^2}\frac{\partial^2}{\partial\varphi^2} + \frac{\partial^2}{\partial z^2}\right] R(\rho)\Phi(\varphi)Z(z) = 0. \qquad (5.1)
\end{aligned}$$

The differential equation of each component in a rectangular coordinate system becomes either $\left[\frac{d^2}{dx^2} + k^2\right] X(x) = 0$ with a real k,

$$\begin{aligned}
X(x) &= A\cos(kx+\alpha) = A\sin(kx+\beta) = A'\cos(kx) + B'\sin(kx) \\
&= Ce^{ikx} + C^*e^{-ikx}, \qquad (5.2)
\end{aligned}$$

or $\left[\frac{d^2}{dz^2} - \kappa^2\right] Z(z) = 0$ with a real κ,

$$Z(z) = Ae^{\kappa z} + Be^{-\kappa z}. \qquad (5.3)$$

For azimuthal angle φ dependent part, $\left[\frac{d^2}{d\varphi^2} + m^2\right]\Phi(\varphi) = 0$ with a real m,

$$\Phi(\varphi) = Ae^{im\varphi} + Be^{-im\varphi}. \qquad (5.4)$$

If $0 \le \varphi \le 2\pi$, m should be an integer for $\Phi(\varphi)$ to be a single valued function. For radial part in a spherical polar coordinate system, $\left[\frac{d^2}{dr^2} - \frac{l(l+1)}{r^2}\right] U(r) = 0$,

$$U(r) = Ar^{l+1} + Br^{-l}. \tag{5.5}$$

For polar angle θ dependent part,

$$\left[\frac{1}{\sin\theta}\frac{d}{d\theta}\sin\theta\frac{d}{d\theta} + \left(l(l+1) - \frac{m^2}{\sin^2\theta}\right)\right] P(\theta) = 0, \tag{5.6}$$

which becomes a generalized Legendre equation with $x = \cos\theta$. For radial part in a cylindrical polar coordinate system,

$$\left[\frac{\partial^2}{\partial\rho^2} + \frac{1}{\rho}\frac{\partial}{\partial\rho} + \left(\kappa^2 - \frac{\nu^2}{\rho^2}\right)\right] R(\rho) = 0, \tag{5.7}$$

which becomes a Bessel equation with $x = \kappa\rho$. The solutions of these differential equations, special functions (특수함수), form a complete set of orthogonal functions for the corresponding variables and has some recursion relations.

For a system with azimuthal symmetry, the differential equation for the polar angle θ becomes Legendre equation with $m = 0$;

$$\frac{d}{dx}\left[(1-x^2)\frac{dP_l(x)}{dx}\right] + l(l+1)P_l(x) = 0 \tag{5.8}$$

with $-1 \le x = \cos\theta \le 1$. The solution $P_l(x)$ is a Legendre polynomial of order l:

$$\begin{aligned}
P_0(x) &= 1, \\
P_1(x) &= x, \\
P_2(x) &= \frac{1}{2}(3x^2 - 1), \\
P_3(x) &= \frac{1}{2}(5x^3 - 3x), \\
P_4(x) &= \frac{1}{8}(35x^4 - 30x^2 + 3), \\
&\vdots
\end{aligned} \tag{5.9}$$

with $P_l(1) = 1$ and the orthogonality condition of

$$\int_{-1}^{1} P_{l'}(x)P_l(x)dx = \frac{2}{2l+1}\delta_{l'l}. \tag{5.10}$$

Some recurrence relations of the Legendre polynomial are

$$(l+1)P_{l+1} - (2l+1)xP_l + lP_{l-1} = 0, \tag{5.11}$$

$$\frac{dP_{l+1}}{dx} - \frac{dP_{l-1}}{dx} - (2l+1)P_l = 0, \tag{5.12}$$

$$\frac{dP_{l+1}}{dx} - x\frac{dP_l}{dx} - (l+1)P_l = 0, \tag{5.13}$$

$$(x^2-1)\frac{dP_l}{dx} - lxP_l + lP_{l-1} = 0. \tag{5.14}$$

The solution of the generalized Legendre equation with $m \neq 0$ $(-1 \leq x \leq 1)$,

$$\frac{d}{dx}\left[(1-x^2)\frac{dP_l^m(x)}{dx}\right] + \left[l(l+1) - \frac{m^2}{1-x^2}\right]P_l^m(x) = 0, \tag{5.15}$$

is called an associated Legendre function $P_l^m(x)$:

$$P_l^m(x) = (-1)^m(1-x^2)^{m/2}\frac{d^m}{dx^m}P_l(x). \tag{5.16}$$

Spherical harmonics is defined by

$$Y_{lm}(\theta,\varphi) = \sqrt{\frac{(2l+1)}{4\pi}\frac{(l-m)!}{(l+m)!}}P_l^m(\cos\theta)e^{im\varphi}. \tag{5.17}$$

The orthonormality condition is

$$\int_0^{\pi}\sin\theta d\theta\int_0^{2\pi}d\varphi Y_{l'm'}^*(\theta,\varphi)Y_{lm}(\theta,\varphi) = \delta_{l'l}\delta_{m'm}. \tag{5.18}$$

The completeness relation is

$$\sum_{l=0}^{\infty}\sum_{m=-l}^{l}Y_{lm}^*(\theta',\varphi')Y_{lm}(\theta,\varphi) = \delta(\cos\theta - \cos\theta')\delta(\varphi-\varphi'). \tag{5.19}$$

The differential equation for the cylindrical radius ρ with $0 \leq x = \kappa\rho$ is the Bessel differential equation;

$$\frac{d^2R_\nu(x)}{dx^2} + \frac{1}{x}\frac{dR_\nu(x)}{dx} + \left(1 - \frac{\nu^2}{x^2}\right)R_\nu(x) = 0. \tag{5.20}$$

The solutions of this equation are the Bessel function $J_\nu(x)$ and Neumann function (Bessel function of the second kind) $N_\nu(x)$;

$$J_\nu(x) = \left(\frac{x}{2}\right)^\nu \sum_{j=0}^{\infty} \frac{(-1)^j}{j!\Gamma(j+\nu+1)} \left(\frac{x}{2}\right)^{2j}, \tag{5.21}$$

$$N_\nu(x) = \frac{J_\nu(x)\cos\nu\pi - J_{-\nu}(x)}{\sin\nu\pi}. \tag{5.22}$$

Hankel functions, Bessel function of the third kind, are defined as

$$\begin{aligned} H_\nu^{(1)}(x) &= J_\nu(x) + iN_\nu(x), \\ H_\nu^{(2)}(x) &= J_\nu(x) - iN_\nu(x). \end{aligned} \tag{5.23}$$

All of these Bessel functions satisfy the recursion formulae

$$R_{\nu-1}(x) + R_{\nu+1}(x) = \frac{2\nu}{x} R_\nu(x), \tag{5.24}$$

$$R_{\nu-1}(x) - R_{\nu+1}(x) = 2\frac{dR_\nu(x)}{dx}. \tag{5.25}$$

If $\kappa^2 = -k^2 < 0$ in Eq.(5.7), then the differential equation becomes

$$\frac{d^2R_\nu(x)}{dx^2} + \frac{1}{x}\frac{dR_\nu(x)}{dx} - \left(1 + \frac{\nu^2}{x^2}\right) R_\nu(x) = 0 \tag{5.26}$$

with $x = k\rho$. The solutions of this equation are modified Bessel functions;

$$\begin{aligned} I_\nu(x) &= i^{-\nu} J_\nu(ix), \\ K_\nu(x) &= \frac{\pi}{2} i^{\nu+1} H_\nu^{(1)}(ix). \end{aligned} \tag{5.27}$$

For Poisson equation $\nabla^2\Psi(\vec{r}) = -k^2\Psi(\vec{r})$ or for time independent Schrödinger equation, the radial part of differential equation in a spherical coordinate system becomes

$$\frac{d^2R(r)}{dr^2} + \frac{2}{r}\frac{dR(r)}{dr} + \left[k^2 - \frac{l(l+1)}{r^2}\right] R(r) = 0, \tag{5.28}$$

compared to Eq.(5.7) of a Laplace equation in a cylindrical coordinate system. With $x = kr$, this becomes

$$\frac{d^2R_\nu(x)}{dx^2} + \frac{2}{x}\frac{dR_\nu(x)}{dx} + \left[1 - \frac{l(l+1)}{x^2}\right] R_\nu(x) = 0 \tag{5.29}$$

and the solutions are the spherical Bessel functions;

$$j_l(x) = \sqrt{\frac{\pi}{2x}} J_{l+1/2}(x), \tag{5.30}$$

$$n_l(x) = \sqrt{\frac{\pi}{2x}} N_{l+1/2}(x). \tag{5.31}$$

To evaluate the value of special function, we may use the corresponding recursion relation starting from the values of the lowest order. Using the recurrence formula of Eq.(5.11), we may evaluate the value of $P_l(x)$ of order l starting from the value of $P_0(x)$ and $P_1(x)$ for a given value of x. Similarly the value of Bessel function of order ν can be found using the recurrence relation Eq.(5.24) starting from $R_0(x)$ and $R_1(x)$. The recursion relation can also be used to evaluate the differential of the special function.

5.2 Gaussian Quadrature; Integral using Special Function

The form of N point numerical integrals in Sect.2.4 are

$$\int_{-1}^{1} f(x)dx \approx \sum_{n=1}^{N} w_n f(x_n). \tag{5.32}$$

As an example, for Simpson's rule of Eq.(2.20),

$$\begin{array}{lll} x_1 = -1, & x_2 = 0, & x_3 = 1; \\ w_1 = 1/3, & w_2 = 4/3, & w_3 = 1/3 \end{array} \tag{5.33}$$

with $N = 3$. For N point integral with equally spaced points, Eq.(5.32) is exact for a polynomial $f(x)$ of order $(N-1)$. Thus the weighting factor w_n can be found from the conditions of

$$\int_a^b x^p dx = \left.\frac{x^{p+1}}{p+1}\right|_a^b = \sum_{n=1}^{N} w_n x_n^p \ ; \quad p = 0, 1, \cdots, (N-1). \tag{5.34}$$

Notice here that x_n does not need to be equally spaced in general.

If we determine x_n together with w_n for N points by condition of Eq.(5.34) with $p = 0, 1, \cdots, (2N-1)$, then Eq.(5.32) is exact for $(2N-1)$-th order polynomial $f(x)$. The x_n can also be determined by using special function.

As an example for integral range of $[a,b]=[-1,1]$, we may use Legendre polynomial $P_N(x)$ of order N. Then any polynomial $f(x)$ of order up to $(2N-1)$ becomes

$$f(x) \quad = \quad Q(x)P_N(x)+R(x) \tag{5.35}$$

with the polynomial $Q(x)$ and $R(x)$ of order up to $(N-1)$. Then the exact integral of $f(x)$ is

$$\int_{-1}^{1} f(x)dx \quad = \quad \int_{-1}^{1} \left[Q(x)P_N(x)+R(x)\right]dx = \int_{-1}^{1} R(x)dx \tag{5.36}$$

due to the orthogonality of Legendre polynomial Eq.(5.10). If we choose N points x_n to be the N zero points of $P_N(x)$, i.e., $P_N(x_n)=0$, then the N point numerical integral of $f(x)$, Eq.(5.32) with Eq.(5.35), is

$$\int_{-1}^{1} f(x)dx \quad \approx \quad \sum_{n=1}^{N} w_n\left[Q(x_n)P_N(x_n)+R(x_n)\right] = \sum_{n=1}^{N} w_nR(x_n). \tag{5.37}$$

Now we only need to determine the value of N weighting factors w_n which can be done by using Eq.(5.34) with $p=0,1,\cdots,(N-1)$. Then

$$w_n \quad = \quad \frac{2}{(1-x_n^2)}\left[\frac{dP_N(x_n)}{dx}\right]^{-2} \tag{5.38}$$

for N points x_n which is the zero point of the Legendre polynomial P_N. This is the Gauss-Legendre quadrature. For $N=3$,

$$\begin{aligned} x_1=-x_3=\sqrt{3/5}, \qquad & x_2=0\ ; \\ w_1=w_3=5/9, \qquad & w_2=8/9. \end{aligned} \tag{5.39}$$

This 3 point Gauss-Legendre quadrature (구적법) has the error of order $O(h^7)$ compared to the error of order $O(h^5)$ of the 3 point Simpson's rule. If the integral range is $[a,b]=[0,\infty]$ then we cannot use Gauss-Legendre quadrature. For such a case we may use other orthogonal special function, such as Laguerre polynomial or Hermite polynomial, depending on the form of $f(x)$ instead of Legendre polynomial.

Chapter 6

Matrix Analysis

Coupled linear equations of N variables

$$\mathsf{A}\mathsf{x} \;=\; \mathsf{b} \tag{6.1}$$

with an $N \times N$ matrix for coefficients A_{ij}

$$\mathsf{A} \;=\; \begin{pmatrix} A_{11} & A_{12} & A_{13} & \cdots & A_{1N} \\ A_{21} & A_{22} & A_{23} & \cdots & A_{2N} \\ \vdots & \vdots & \vdots & \ddots & \\ A_{N1} & A_{N2} & A_{N3} & \cdots & A_{NN} \end{pmatrix}, \tag{6.2}$$

and $N \times 1$ column vectors for variables x_i and constants b_i

$$\mathsf{x} \;=\; \begin{pmatrix} x_1 \\ x_2 \\ x_3 \\ \vdots \\ x_N \end{pmatrix}, \qquad \mathsf{b} \;=\; \begin{pmatrix} b_1 \\ b_2 \\ b_3 \\ \vdots \\ b_N \end{pmatrix}. \tag{6.3}$$

Second order differential equation

$$\frac{d^2y(x)}{dx^2} + k^2(x)y(x) = S(x) \tag{6.4}$$

in a discretized grid space $x_1, x_2, \cdots, x_N$ with a grid spacing of h can be expressed by a matrix equation with

$$\mathsf{A} = \begin{pmatrix} -\frac{2}{h^2}+k_1^2 & \frac{1}{h^2} & 0 & \cdots & & & \\ \frac{1}{h^2} & -\frac{2}{h^2}+k_2^2 & \frac{1}{h^2} & \cdots & & & \\ 0 & \frac{1}{h^2} & -\frac{2}{h^2}+k_3^2 & \cdots & & & \\ \vdots & \ddots & \ddots & \ddots & & & \\ & & & \cdots & \frac{1}{h^2} & -\frac{2}{h^2}+k_{N-1}^2 & \frac{1}{h^2} \\ & & & \cdots & 0 & \frac{1}{h^2} & -\frac{2}{h^2}+k_N^2 \end{pmatrix},$$

$$\mathsf{x} = \begin{pmatrix} y(x_1) \\ y(x_2) \\ y(x_3) \\ \vdots \\ y(x_{N-1}) \\ y(x_N) \end{pmatrix}, \qquad \mathsf{b} = \begin{pmatrix} S(x_1) \\ S(x_2) \\ S(x_3) \\ \vdots \\ S(x_{N-1}) \\ S(x_N) \end{pmatrix}, \tag{6.5}$$

and $k_n = k(x_n)$. Here the $N \times N$ matrix A is a tri-diagonal matrix.

6.1 Matrix Inversion

The solution of Eq.(6.1) is

$$\mathsf{x} = \mathsf{A}^{-1}\mathsf{b} \tag{6.6}$$

with the inverse matrix A^{-1}. The determinant of the matrix A should be non-zero for the inverse matrix A^{-1} to exist. Inverse matrix can be found using Gauss-Jordan method: Change matrix A and unit matrix I ($I_{ij} = \delta_{ij}$) in the same way until matrix A changed to unit matrix I, i.e.,

$$\mathsf{T_i} \cdots \mathsf{T_j T_k A} = \mathsf{I} \quad : \quad \mathsf{T_i} \cdots \mathsf{T_j T_k I} = \mathsf{A}^{-1}. \tag{6.7}$$

The matrices $\mathsf{T_i}$ are, for 5×5 matrix as an example,

$$\mathsf{T}_1 = \begin{pmatrix} 1 & 0 & 0 & 0 & 0 \\ 0 & 1 & 0 & 0 & 0 \\ 0 & 0 & a & 0 & 0 \\ 0 & 0 & 0 & 1 & 0 \\ 0 & 0 & 0 & 0 & 1 \end{pmatrix},$$

$$\mathsf{T_2} = \begin{pmatrix} 0 & 0 & 0 & 1 & 0 \\ 0 & 1 & 0 & 0 & 0 \\ 0 & 0 & 1 & 0 & 0 \\ 1 & 0 & 0 & 0 & 0 \\ 0 & 0 & 0 & 0 & 1 \end{pmatrix}, \tag{6.8}$$

$$\mathsf{T_3} = \begin{pmatrix} 1 & 0 & 0 & 0 & 0 \\ 0 & 1 & 0 & 0 & 0 \\ 0 & 0 & 1 & 0 & 0 \\ 0 & b & 0 & 1 & 0 \\ 0 & 0 & 0 & 0 & 1 \end{pmatrix},$$

$$\mathsf{A} = \begin{pmatrix} A_{11} & A_{12} & A_{13} & A_{14} & A_{15} \\ A_{21} & A_{22} & A_{23} & A_{24} & A_{25} \\ A_{31} & A_{32} & A_{33} & A_{34} & A_{35} \\ A_{41} & A_{42} & A_{43} & A_{44} & A_{45} \\ A_{51} & A_{52} & A_{53} & A_{54} & A_{55} \end{pmatrix}.$$

Multiplying $\mathsf{T_i}$ to A from left

$$\mathsf{T_1A} = \begin{pmatrix} A_{11} & A_{12} & A_{13} & A_{14} & A_{15} \\ A_{21} & A_{22} & A_{23} & A_{24} & A_{25} \\ aA_{31} & aA_{32} & aA_{33} & aA_{34} & aA_{35} \\ A_{41} & A_{42} & A_{43} & A_{44} & A_{45} \\ A_{51} & A_{52} & A_{53} & A_{54} & A_{55} \end{pmatrix},$$

$$\mathsf{T_2A} = \begin{pmatrix} A_{41} & A_{42} & A_{43} & A_{44} & A_{45} \\ A_{21} & A_{22} & A_{23} & A_{24} & A_{25} \\ A_{31} & A_{32} & A_{33} & A_{34} & A_{35} \\ A_{11} & A_{12} & A_{13} & A_{14} & A_{15} \\ A_{51} & A_{52} & A_{53} & A_{54} & A_{55} \end{pmatrix}, \tag{6.9}$$

$$\mathsf{T_3A} = \begin{pmatrix} A_{11} & A_{12} & A_{13} & A_{14} & A_{15} \\ A_{21} & A_{22} & A_{23} & A_{24} & A_{25} \\ A_{31} & A_{32} & A_{33} & A_{34} & A_{35} \\ A_{41}+bA_{21} & A_{42}+bA_{22} & A_{43}+bA_{23} & A_{44}+bA_{24} & A_{45}+bA_{25} \\ A_{51} & A_{52} & A_{53} & A_{54} & A_{55} \end{pmatrix}.$$

Multiplying $\mathsf{T_1}$ from left changes A to a new matrix with elements in 3rd row multiplied by a. $\mathsf{T_2}$ changes A to a new matrix with 1st row and 4th row exchanged. $\mathsf{T_3}$ add b times the elements of 2nd row to the elements of the 4th row of A. Multiplying T_i to A from right

$$\begin{aligned}
\mathsf{AT}_1 &= \begin{pmatrix} A_{11} & A_{12} & aA_{13} & A_{14} & A_{15} \\ A_{21} & A_{22} & aA_{23} & A_{24} & A_{25} \\ A_{31} & A_{32} & aA_{33} & A_{34} & A_{35} \\ A_{41} & A_{42} & aA_{43} & A_{44} & A_{45} \\ A_{51} & A_{52} & aA_{53} & A_{54} & A_{55} \end{pmatrix}, \\
\mathsf{AT}_2 &= \begin{pmatrix} A_{14} & A_{12} & A_{13} & A_{11} & A_{15} \\ A_{24} & A_{22} & A_{23} & A_{21} & A_{25} \\ A_{34} & A_{32} & A_{33} & A_{31} & A_{35} \\ A_{44} & A_{42} & A_{43} & A_{41} & A_{45} \\ A_{54} & A_{52} & A_{53} & A_{51} & A_{55} \end{pmatrix}, \\
\mathsf{AT}_3 &= \begin{pmatrix} A_{11} & A_{12}+bA_{14} & A_{13} & A_{14} & A_{15} \\ A_{21} & A_{22}+bA_{24} & A_{23} & A_{24} & A_{25} \\ A_{31} & A_{32}+bA_{34} & A_{33} & A_{34} & A_{35} \\ A_{41} & A_{42}+bA_{44} & A_{43} & A_{44} & A_{45} \\ A_{51} & A_{52}+bA_{54} & A_{53} & A_{54} & A_{55} \end{pmatrix}.
\end{aligned} \tag{6.10}$$

AT_1 multiplies a to the elements in 3rd column of A. AT_2 exchanges elements in 1st column and 4th column. AT_3 add b times the element in 4th column to the element in the 2nd column.

To find the inverse matrix of A, change A and I in the same way by exchanging two rows, multiplying a constant to one row, or multiplying a constant to one row and add the result to some other row until A changed to a unit matrix I. During this process, keep diagonal element (called pivot element) non-zero by exchanging two rows or columns if necessary.

6.2 Eigenvalue Problem

For some special vector $\mathsf{x} = \phi_n$ in Eq.(6.1), the vector $\mathsf{b} = \mathsf{A}\phi_n$ becomes the vector ϕ_n times a constant λ_n. Thus, the eigenvalue equation for $N \times N$ matrix A is

$$\mathsf{A}\phi_n = \lambda_n \phi_n \tag{6.11}$$

with eigenvalue λ_n and eigenvector ϕ_n. Eigenvector ϕ_n can have an arbitrary norm and we usually normalize the norm to be 1. The determinant of $(\mathsf{A}-\lambda\mathsf{I})$

should be zero at $\lambda = \lambda_n$, i.e.,

$$P_A(\lambda) = |\mathsf{A} - \lambda\mathsf{I}| = \prod_{n=1}^{N} (\lambda_n - \lambda) = 0. \tag{6.12}$$

For a tri-diagonal matrix A,

$$P_A(\lambda) = \begin{vmatrix} A_{11}-\lambda & A_{12} & 0 & 0 & 0 & \cdots & & & \\ A_{21} & A_{22}-\lambda & A_{23} & 0 & 0 & \cdots & & & \\ 0 & A_{32} & A_{33}-\lambda & A_{34} & 0 & \cdots & & & \\ & & \cdots & & & & & & \\ & & & & & \cdots & 0 & A_{NN-1} & A_{NN}-\lambda \end{vmatrix}$$

This determinant can be found recursively as

$$\begin{aligned} P_1(\lambda) &= A_{11} - \lambda, \\ P_2(\lambda) &= (A_{22} - \lambda)P_1(\lambda) - A_{12}A_{21}, \\ P_3(\lambda) &= (A_{33} - \lambda)P_2(\lambda) - A_{23}A_{32}P_1(\lambda), \\ &\cdots \\ P_n(\lambda) &= (A_{nn} - \lambda)P_{n-1}(\lambda) - A_{nn-1}A_{n-1n}P_{n-2}(\lambda). \end{aligned} \tag{6.13}$$

We may need only few eigenvalues for a large N. Then use $P_n(\lambda) = 0$ with n large enough but much smaller than N.

For a symmetric or Hermitian matrix, eigenvalues are real and eigenvectors are orthogonal.

6.3 Inverse Vector Iteration

Inverse vector iteration is one of simple methods of finding eigenvector ϕ_n of a matrix A for a given eigenvalue λ_n. For the eigenvector ϕ_n of a matrix A,

$$[\mathsf{A} - (\lambda_n + \epsilon)\mathsf{I}]\,\phi_n = -\epsilon\phi_n$$

with an arbitrary constant ϵ. However if ϕ is not the eigenvector ϕ_n then

$$[\mathsf{A} - (\lambda_n + \epsilon)\mathsf{I}]\,\phi = c\phi' \neq -\epsilon\phi$$

in general. Using these facts, the eigenvector ϕ_n for a given eigenvalue λ_n of matrix A can be found iteratively as

$$\phi_n^{(2)} = C\left[\mathsf{A} - (\lambda_n + \epsilon)\mathsf{I}\right]^{-1} \phi_n^{(1)} \tag{6.14}$$

together with normalization condition. Start with an arbitrarily chosen but normalized vector $\phi_n^{(1)}$, then iterate Eq.(6.14) until the new vector $\phi_n^{(2)}$ converges to the old vector $\phi_n^{(1)}$ within allowed error. Without the relaxation parameter ϵ, inverse of $[\mathsf{A} - \lambda_n \mathsf{I}]$ does not exists for eigenvector ϕ_n.

6.4 Damped Gradient Iteration

For a matrix $\mathsf{H} = \mathsf{T} + \mathsf{V}$ with eigenvalue ω,

$$\begin{aligned} \psi' &= \psi - d[K_0\mathsf{I} + \mathsf{T}]^{-1}(\mathsf{H} - \omega)\psi \\ &= \psi - \epsilon[\mathsf{I} + \mathsf{T}/K_0]^{-1}(\mathsf{H} - \omega)\psi. \end{aligned} \tag{6.15}$$

If ψ is the eigenvector of H with eigenvalue ω, then $\psi' = \psi$. The damping constant K_0 is used to stabilize the components with small kinetic energy $\mathsf{T} = C\nabla^2$ and ϵ is a relaxation parameter. The value of K_0 must be roughly the depth of the potential V. Start with a cleverly chosen ψ and get new ψ by normalizing ψ'. Iterate this step until ψ converges.

6.5 Lanczos Algorithm

For an arbitrary vector x, $\mathsf{x}_n = \mathsf{A}^n\mathsf{x}$ becomes eigenvector of A with largest eigenvalue for a large n. With a proper unitary matrix U, $\mathsf{A} = \mathsf{U}\mathrm{diag}(\lambda_i)\mathsf{U}^\dagger$ and $\mathsf{A}^n = \mathsf{U}\mathrm{diag}(\lambda_i^n)\mathsf{U}^\dagger$.

To find some lowest eigenvalues for a large symmetric matrix, approximate a large matrix A by a tridiagonal matrix in a smaller basis space. Choose basis vectors as,

$$\begin{aligned} &\psi_1, \\ \psi_2 &= C_2(\mathsf{A}\psi_1 - A_{11}\psi_1), \\ \psi_3 &= C_3(\mathsf{A}\psi_2 - A_{22}\psi_2 - A_{21}\psi_1), \\ &\cdots \\ \psi_{n+1} &= C_{n+1}(\mathsf{A}\psi_n - A_{nn}\psi_n - A_{nn-1}\psi_{n-1}) \end{aligned} \tag{6.16}$$

with normalization constants of

$$\begin{aligned}
C_2 &= [(\mathsf{A}\psi_1)^t(\mathsf{A}\psi_1) - (A_{11})^2]^{-1/2}, \\
C_3 &= [(\mathsf{A}\psi_2)^t(\mathsf{A}\psi_2) - (A_{22})^2 - (A_{21})^2]^{-1/2}, \\
\cdots \\
C_{n+1} &= [(\mathsf{A}\psi_n)^t(\mathsf{A}\psi_n) - (A_{nn})^2 - (A_{nn-1})^2]^{-1/2}
\end{aligned} \tag{6.17}$$

where $A_{nm} = \psi_n^t \mathsf{A}\psi_m$ and ψ_{i-1}, ψ_i, and ψ_{i+1} are orthogonal. The first vector ψ_1 should not be an eigenvector of the matrix A. Then approximate the large matrix A with smaller tridiagonal matrix with elements $A_{nm} = \psi_n^t \mathsf{A}\psi_\mathsf{m}$. Using this small tridiagonal matrix, find even smaller number of eigenvectors and eigenvalues for lowest eigenvalues.

Gram-Schmidt orthogonalization of vectors. For vectors ϕ_1, ϕ_2, $\cdots$, ϕ_N,

$$\begin{aligned}
\psi_1 &= C_1\phi_1, \\
\psi_2 &= C_2(\phi_2 - \psi_1\psi_1^t\phi_2), \\
\psi_3 &= C_3(\phi_3 - \psi_2\psi_2^t\phi_3 - \psi_1\psi_1^t\phi_3), \\
\cdots \\
\psi_n &= C_n\left(\phi_n - \sum_{i=1}^{n-1}\psi_i\psi_i^t\phi_n\right), \\
\cdots \\
\psi_N &= C_N\left(\phi_N - \sum_{i=1}^{N-1}\psi_i\psi_i^t\phi_N\right).
\end{aligned} \tag{6.18}$$

The new vectors ψ_n are orthonormal with proper normalization constant C_n.

Chapter 7

Discretized Grid Space in Higher Dimension

Poisson equation $\nabla^2\Phi(\vec{r}) = -S(\vec{r})$ or time independent Schrödinger equation

$$\left[-\frac{\hbar^2}{2m}\nabla^2 + V(\vec{r})\right]\psi(\vec{r}) \quad = \quad E\psi(\vec{r})$$

in 2-dimensional space is an Elliptic differential equation

$$\left[\frac{\partial^2}{\partial x^2} + \frac{\partial^2}{\partial y^2}\right]\Phi(x,y) \quad = \quad -k^2(x,y)\Phi(x,y) - S(x,y). \tag{7.1}$$

Wave equation

$$\frac{\partial^2}{\partial t^2}\Psi(\vec{r},t) \quad = \quad v^2\nabla^2\Psi(\vec{r},t)$$

in 1-dimensional spatial space is a Parabolic differential equation

$$\left[\frac{\partial^2}{\partial x^2} - \frac{\partial^2}{\partial y^2}\right]\Phi(x,y) \quad = \quad -k^2(x,y)\Phi(x,y) - S(x,y). \tag{7.2}$$

Both the elliptic and parabolic differential equations have second order differential in all variables x and y and the same numerical method can be used. Time dependent Schrödinger equation or diffusion equation,

$$
\begin{aligned}
i\hbar\frac{\partial}{\partial t}\psi(\vec{r},t) &= \left[-\frac{\hbar^2}{2m}\nabla^2 + V(\vec{r})\right]\psi(\vec{r},t), \\
\frac{\partial}{\partial t}\Phi(\vec{r},t) &= \vec{\nabla}\cdot\left[D(\vec{r})\vec{\nabla}\Phi(\vec{r},t)\right] + S(\vec{r},t),
\end{aligned}
$$

in 1-dimensional spatial space is a Hyperbolic differential equation

$$
\frac{\partial}{\partial t}\phi(x,t) = D(x,t)\frac{\partial^2}{\partial x^2}\phi(x,t) - K(x,t)\phi(x,t) + S(x,t). \tag{7.3}
$$

The hyperbolic differential equation has first order differential for one variable and second order differential for other variables. Numerical methods for 3-dimension are simple extension of numerical methods in 2-dimensional space.

7.1 Discretization and Variational Principle

There are some ambiguity in discretizing spatial space. For example, for the differential equation $\vec{\nabla}\cdot[D\vec{\nabla}\phi] = -S$, the value of x-component of $\vec{\nabla}\phi$ corresponds to the point which is the midpoint of grid points in x direction but on the grid point itself in y direction while the value of y-component of $\vec{\nabla}\phi$ corresponds to the point which is the midpoint of grid points in y direction but on the grid point itself in x direction. Thus the value of D is also needed to be evaluated at different point depending on which component it belongs. This can be clarified with variational principle. The equation $\vec{\nabla}\cdot[D\vec{\nabla}\phi] = -S$ can be derived from the corresponding functional

$$
E = \int d^3r\left[\frac{1}{2}D(\vec{\nabla}\phi)^2 - S\phi\right] \tag{7.4}
$$

by using variational method with respect to the function ϕ. To find $\phi(\vec{r})$ which minimizes the value of the functional E, vary E with respect to the function ϕ by using $\phi + \delta\phi$. The first order in $\delta\phi(\vec{r})$ is

$$
\begin{aligned}
&\int_V d^3r\left[\frac{1}{2}D(\vec{r})\nabla\phi(\vec{r})\cdot\vec{\nabla}\delta\phi(\vec{r}) - S(\vec{r})\delta\phi(\vec{r})\right] \\
&\quad = \int_V d^3r\left[-\vec{\nabla}\cdot D(\vec{r})\nabla\phi(\vec{r}) - S(\vec{r})\right]\delta\phi(\vec{r}) = 0
\end{aligned} \tag{7.5}
$$

for arbitrary variation $\delta\phi(\vec{r})$ with $\delta\phi = 0$ at the boundary surface due to the boundary condition of the differential equation. Thus we finally get the differential equation $\vec{\nabla} \cdot \left[D\vec{\nabla}\phi(\vec{r})\right] = -S(\vec{r})$. Actually this equation is the condition for the extremum of E.

In 2-dimensional space,

$$\frac{\partial}{\partial x}\left(D\frac{\partial\phi}{\partial x}\right) + \frac{\partial}{\partial y}\left(D\frac{\partial\phi}{\partial y}\right) = -S(x,y), \tag{7.6}$$

$$\frac{1}{2}\int dx \int dy \frac{\partial\phi}{\partial x} D \frac{\partial\phi}{\partial x} + \frac{1}{2}\int dx \int dy \frac{\partial\phi}{\partial y} D \frac{\partial\phi}{\partial y} - \int dx \int dy S(x,y)\phi(x,y) = 0. \tag{7.7}$$

In Eq.(7.6), every terms should be evaluated at a same point while in Eq.(7.7) each term can be integrated separately independent to the other terms. Thus convert Eq.(7.4) into discretized space by evaluating each term separately independent of other terms and then use variational method to obtain the difference equation for ϕ_{ij} in the grid space.

7.2 Boundary Value Problem

Consider boundary condition for a difference equation in 2-dimensional grid space such as discretized elliptic equation

$$\frac{\phi_{i+1j} - 2\phi_{ij} + \phi_{i-1j}}{\Delta x^2} + \frac{\phi_{ij+1} - 2\phi_{ij} + \phi_{ij-1}}{\Delta y^2} = -S_{ij}$$

for the grid sizes of Δx and Δy. This is simplified as

$$4\phi_{ij} - \phi_{i+1j} - \phi_{i-1j} - \phi_{ij+1} - \phi_{ij-1} = h^2 S_{ij}$$

for the case of $\Delta x = \Delta y = h$.

For Dirichlet boundary condition, the values of function at the boundary are given; ϕ_{1j}, ϕ_{Nj}, ϕ_{i1}, and ϕ_{iN}. The boundary condition incorporates with the difference equation as

$$4\phi_{iN-1} - \phi_{i+1N-1} - \phi_{i-1N-1} - \phi_{iN-2} = h^2 S_{iN-1} + \phi_{iN} \tag{7.8}$$

for ϕ_{iN} as an example. The values on the right hand side are known from the value of the source and the Dirichlet boundary condition of the function. The values on the left side should be determined by numerical method.

For Neumann boundary condition, the normal component of gradient at the boundary are given; for example $\partial\phi/\partial y = g(x)$ are given at the boundary of $y = y_N$ which becomes

$$\phi_{iN} - \phi_{iN-1} = hg_i \tag{7.9}$$

in the grid space. Then the difference equation becomes

$$3\phi_{iN-1} - \phi_{i+1N-1} - \phi_{i-1N-1}\phi_{iN-2} = h^2 S_{iN-1} + hg_i \tag{7.10}$$

at the boundary (x_i, y_N). The values on the right hand side are known from the value of the source and the Neumann boundary condition Eq.(7.9) of the function. The values on the left side should be determined by numerical method.

7.3 Iterative Gauss-Seidel Method

For an elliptic or parabolic difference equation, iterative Gauss-Seidel method can be used. For $\nabla^2\phi = -S$, the difference equation in 1-dimensional grid space is

$$\phi_{i+1} - 2\phi_i + \phi_{i-1} = -h^2 S_i$$

for ϕ_i which is the solution of the differential equation. The Gauss-Seidel iteration Method for this case is

$$\phi_i' = (1-\omega)\phi_i + \frac{\omega}{2}[\phi_{i+1} + \phi_{i-1} + h^2 S_i]. \tag{7.11}$$

Use old values ϕ_i to evaluate the value of ϕ_i' and renew the value of ϕ_i with the value of ϕ_i' for every grid points i except for the boundary points. Repeat this procedure until ϕ_i' and ϕ_i agrees within a permitted error range. Most recently evaluated values of ϕ_i's can be used in the right hand side at each step. For 2-dimensional difference equation

$$4\phi_{ij} - \phi_{i+1j} - \phi_{i-1j} - \phi_{ij+1} - \phi_{ij-1} = h^2 S_{ij}$$

the iterative Gauss-Seidel method is

$$\phi_{ij}' = (1-\omega)\phi_{ij} + \frac{\omega}{4}[\phi_{i+1j} + \phi_{i-1j}\phi_{ij+1} + \phi_{ij-1} + h^2 S_{ij}]. \tag{7.12}$$

Choose the relaxation parameter ω to be some value between $0 < \omega < 1$ for the faster convergence. To use iterative Gauss-Seidel method we should assume some function for ϕ to start the iteration steps. Properly guessed values of ϕ on the grid points as a starting value reduces iteration step number very much.

7.4 Gaussian Elimination

Diffusion equation and time dependent Schrödinger equation are examples of hyperbolic differential equation;

$$\begin{aligned} \frac{\partial \phi(\vec{r},t)}{\partial t} &= \vec{\nabla}\cdot\left[D(\vec{r},t)\vec{\nabla}\phi(\vec{r},t)\right] - K(\vec{r},t)\phi(\vec{r},t) + S(\vec{r},t) \\ &= -H\phi(\vec{r},t) + S(\vec{r},t). \end{aligned} \tag{7.13}$$

A hyperbolic differential equation has first order differential for one variable t while second order differential for other variables $\vec{r}$. The discretization of H in a spatial grid space is the same as for the case of elliptic or parabolic differential equation.

At a discretized time step $t_n = n\Delta t$ for one spatial dimension

$$\frac{\phi_i^{n+1} - \phi_i^n}{\Delta t} = -(H\phi)_i + S_i^n. \tag{7.14}$$

Evaluating ϕ in the right hand side of Eq.(7.14) on the spatial grid point x_i at time t_n, explicit differencing scheme becomes

$$\phi^{n+1} = (1 - H\Delta t)\phi^n + S^n\Delta t. \tag{7.15}$$

The right hand side is evaluated at time t_n.

In implicit scheme, by evaluating ϕ in the right hand side of Eq.(7.14) at time t_{n+1},

$$\begin{aligned} \frac{\phi_i^{n+1} - \phi_i^n}{\Delta t} &= -(H\phi^{n+1})_i + S_i^n, \\ \phi^{n+1} &= \frac{1}{1 + H\Delta t}[\phi^n + S^n\Delta t], \end{aligned} \tag{7.16}$$

or by evaluating ϕ in the right hand side of Eq.(7.14) as the average of ϕ^{n+1} and ϕ^n,

$$\begin{aligned}
\frac{\phi_i^{n+1} - \phi_i^n}{\Delta t} &= -\left(H\left[\frac{\phi^{n+1}+\phi^n}{2}\right]\right)_i + S_i^n, \\
\phi^{n+1} &= \frac{1}{1+\frac{1}{2}H\Delta t}\left[\left(1-\frac{1}{2}H\Delta t\right)\phi^n + S^n\Delta t\right]. \qquad (7.17)
\end{aligned}$$

The right hand side are all known quantity at time t_n. However matrix inversion appears as $\phi^{n+1} = \mathsf{A}^{-1}\mathsf{b}^n$ in implicit scheme.

Gaussian elimination method to find ϕ of $\mathsf{A}\phi = \mathsf{b}$ for tri-diagonal matrix;

$$A_i^-\phi_{i-1}^{n+1} + A_i^0\phi_i^{n+1} + A_i^+\phi_{i+1}^{n+1} = b_i^n, \qquad (7.18)$$

which is a three point recurrence relation for ϕ^{n+1} with the known functions A_i and b_i. As an example,

$$\begin{aligned}
b_i^n &= \phi_i^n + S_i^n\Delta t, \\
A_i^0 &= 1 + \frac{2}{h^2}\Delta t, \qquad (7.19) \\
A_i^\pm &= -\frac{\Delta t}{h^2}
\end{aligned}$$

for Eq.(7.16) with $H = -\frac{d^2}{dx^2}$ and the grid size h. Using a forward two point recurrence relation for ϕ^{n+1},

$$\phi_{i+1}^{n+1} = \alpha_i\phi_i^{n+1} + \beta_i, \qquad (7.20)$$

Eq.(7.18) becomes

$$\begin{aligned}
A_i^-\phi_{i-1} + A_i^0\phi_i + A_i^+(\alpha_i\phi_i + \beta_i) &= b_i, \\
\phi_i &= \gamma_i A_i^-\phi_{i-1} + \gamma_i(A_i^+\beta_i - b_i),
\end{aligned}$$

which gives backward two point recurrence relations

$$\begin{aligned}
\alpha_{i-1} &= \gamma_i A_i^-, \\
\beta_{i-1} &= \gamma_i(A_i^+\beta_i - b_i), \qquad (7.21) \\
\gamma_i &= -\frac{1}{A_i^0 + A_i^+\alpha_i}.
\end{aligned}$$

The boundary condition for α and β at x_{N-1} are

$$\begin{aligned} \alpha_{N-1} &= 0, \\ \beta_{N-1} &= \phi_N, \end{aligned} \tag{7.22}$$

which come from the boundary condition ϕ_N at x_N

$$\phi_N = \alpha_{N-1}\phi_{N-1} + \beta_{N-1}.$$

The Gaussian elimination method is composed with a forward two point recursion relation Eq.(7.20) starting with boundary condition ϕ_1 and backward two point recurrence relations Eq.(7.21) starting with boundary condition ϕ_N through Eq.(7.22).

In 2-d H is not tridiagonal such as

$$\begin{aligned} (H\phi)_{ij} &= -(\nabla^2\phi)_{ij} \\ &= -\frac{1}{h^2}\left(\phi_{i+1j} - 2\phi_{ij} + \phi_{i-1j} + \phi_{ij+1} - 2\phi_{ij} + \phi_{ij-1}\right). \end{aligned} \tag{7.23}$$

If we separate as

$$H = H_x + H_y \tag{7.24}$$

for each coordinate, then

$$[1 + H_x\Delta t + H_y\Delta t]\phi^{n+1} \approx [1 + H_x\Delta t][1 + H_y\Delta t]\phi^{n+1} = \phi^n + S^n\Delta t \tag{7.25}$$

for implicit scheme. Thus

$$\phi^{n+1} = \left[\frac{1}{1 + H_x\Delta t}\right]\left[\frac{1}{1 + H_y\Delta t}\right][\phi^n + S^n\Delta t],$$

which is

$$\begin{aligned} \phi^{n+1/2} &= \frac{1}{[1 + H_y\Delta t]}[\phi^n + S^n\Delta t], \\ \phi^{n+1} &= \frac{1}{[1 + H_x\Delta t]}\phi^{n+1/2}. \end{aligned} \tag{7.26}$$

The matrix H_i in each of these equation is now tridiagonal.

Gaussian elimination method can also be used for an elliptical differential equation with source term such as

$$(H_x + H_y)\phi \;=\; S \tag{7.27}$$

in 2-d. Using acceleration parameter ω

$$(H_x + H_y + \omega)\phi = S + \omega\phi,$$

which becomes

$$\begin{aligned} \phi^{n+1/2} &= \frac{1}{(\omega + H_x)}[S - (H_y - \omega)\phi^n], \\ \phi^{n+1} &= \frac{1}{(\omega + H_y)}[S - (H_x - \omega)\phi^{n+1/2}]. \end{aligned} \tag{7.28}$$

Iterate these equation starting with a guessed function ϕ^1. The matrices H_i for each component are tridiagonal and thus the Gaussian elimination method can be used for matrix inversion.

Chapter 8

Monte-Carlo Simulation

For scattering, each collision occurs randomly. For integral in high dimension, the number of grid points becomes very large even if each component has small number of grid points. A system with very high degree of freedom is able to be treated only by statistical method. In statistical physics partition function for a system of N particles is

$$Q = \int d^3r_1 d^3r_2 \cdots d^3r_N \exp\left[-\beta\left(\sum_i \frac{p_i^2}{2m_i} + \sum_{i<j} V(\vec{r}_i - \vec{r}_j)\right)\right]. \quad (8.1)$$

Brownian motion of pollen may be described by random walk.

8.1 Monte-Carlo Method

Numerical integral in 1-dimension is approximated as

$$I = \int_0^1 f(x)dx \approx \frac{1}{N}\sum_{i=1}^{N} f(x_i) = I_N \quad (8.2)$$

for equally spaced grid with size $h = 1/N$. In a Monte-Carlo method N points are chosen randomly between $0 \le x \le 1$. The error σ_I of Monte-Carlo integral I_N is, from Eq.(10.6),

$$\sigma_I^2 = |I - I_N|^2 = \frac{\sigma_f^2}{N} = \frac{1}{N-1}\left[\frac{1}{N}\sum_{i=1}^{N} f_i^2 - \left(\frac{1}{N}\sum_{i=1}^{N} f_i\right)^2\right]. \quad (8.3)$$

The standard deviation σ_I of I_N is smaller for larger N with $N^{-1/2}$. For a large N, the randomly chosen x_i are distributed uniformly between $0 \leq x_i \leq 1$. The integral I_N for a slowly varying smooth function $f(x)$ converges to the exact integral I fast with smaller N than for a fast varying function.

For integral in d-dimensional space, each point is randomly picked by a set of d random values. As an example

$$\pi = 4\int_0^1 dx \int_0^1 dy \theta(1-x^2-y^2) \approx 4\frac{1}{N}\sum_{i=1}^{N} \theta(1-x_i^2-y_i^2) \quad (8.4)$$

where $\theta(r)$ is a step function which is 1 for $r > 0$ and is 0 for $r < 0$. The random points (x_i, y_i) are picked by a pair of random numbers x_i and y_i between 0 and 1. This integral can also be done by throwing coins. Draw a square of side 1 m and draw a quarter circle of radius 1 m centered at one corner of the square. Then throw coins blindly to the square. The ratio of the total number of coins landed in the quarter circle to the number of coins landed in the square is the value of the integral.

If a function $f(x)$ can be factorized to a slowly varying function and a well known positive weighting function $w(x)$ with

$$\int_0^1 w(x)dx = 1 \quad (8.5)$$

the integral can be rewritten as

$$I = \int_0^1 dx f(x) = \int_0^1 dx w(x)\frac{f(x)}{w(x)} = \int_0^1 dy \frac{f(x(y))}{w(x(y))} \quad (8.6)$$

where

$$y(x) = \int_0^x dx w(x) \quad (8.7)$$

which is a solution of

$$\frac{dy(x)}{dx} = w(x) \quad (8.8)$$

with the boundary condition of $y(0) = 0$ and $y(1) = 1$. Then

$$I \approx \frac{1}{N}\sum_{i=1}^{N} \frac{f(x(y_i))}{w(x(y_i))} \quad (8.9)$$

with random number y_i distributed uniformly in $0 \leq y_i \leq 1$.

For an uniformly distributed y_i, the random number $x_i = x(y_i)$ are distributed in the form of function $w(x)$ which is a non-uniform distribution. If the function $w(x)$ has an analytical inverse function $w^{-1}(y)$ then the distribution of the random number $x_i = w^{-1}(y_i)$ is $w(x)$. If $w(x)$ has no analytical inverse then we can use numerical method to find non-uniformly distributed x_i from uniformly distributed y_i. Choose uniformly distributed M values by $y_i = i/M$ in order with $i = 1, 2, \cdots, M$. Then use $\frac{dy}{dx} = w(x)$ to find $x_i(y_i)$ numerically as

$$x_{i+1} = x_i + \frac{y_{i+1} - y_i}{w(x_i)} = x_i + \frac{1}{Mw(x_i)}. \tag{8.10}$$

For random number y which is different from one of the y_i, the corresponding random number x can be found using interpolation with $y_i < y < y_{i+1}$.

8.2 Metropolis Algorithm

Random walk in an empty street requires only one random number for each step. However in a crowded street of metropolis, the realization of next step depends on the occupancy by other person at the next step. The state of scattered particle in a collision of projectile from a target depends on the differential scattering cross section between projectile and target.

For a random walk in a street with a probability density $w(x)$ each step depends on $w(x)$. To move from position x_n to next step x_{n+1} pick x_t by a random number. If

$$r = \frac{w(x_t)}{w(x_n)} \tag{8.11}$$

is larger than 1 then x_t is the next step $x_{n+1} = x_t$ since the probability density at x_t is larger than the probability density at x_n. However, in metropolis Monte-Carlo algorithm, the position x_t is allowed as the next step x_{n+1} if r is larger than a new random number $\eta < 1$ even if $r < 1$. If $r < \eta$ then x_t is not allowed as next step and thus $x_{n+1} = x_n$. In overall randomly chosen new position x_t becomes the next step, i.e., $x_{n+1} = x_t$ if $r > \eta$ and $x_{n+1} = x_n$ without moving to a new position if $r < \eta$ where η is another random number in $0 \leq \eta \leq 1$.

Chapter 9

Computer and Experiment

9.1 Computer in Experiment

- Data Acquisition ; Acquire experimental data from experimental equipment and store in computer.
- Data Analysis ; Analyze the raw data to get physical data.
- Equipment Control ; Use the analyzed data to send controlling signal to experimental equipment. Useful not only for convenience but also for experiments at remote place or in an extreme environment such as very hot place, radioactive place, etc.

9.2 Connection of Computer and Experimental Equipment

- Interface ; General Purpose Interface Bus (GPIB) Board, USB.
- D/A Converter ; Convert a digital signal in computer to an analog signal to control experimental device.

  A simple D/A converter is a binary weighted resister D/A converter as shown in Fig.9.1 for 4-bit digital data. The current flowing through switch S_n is $2^{n-1}I_0$ when the switch is closed. The total current flowing through switches which are closed or opened according to the binary

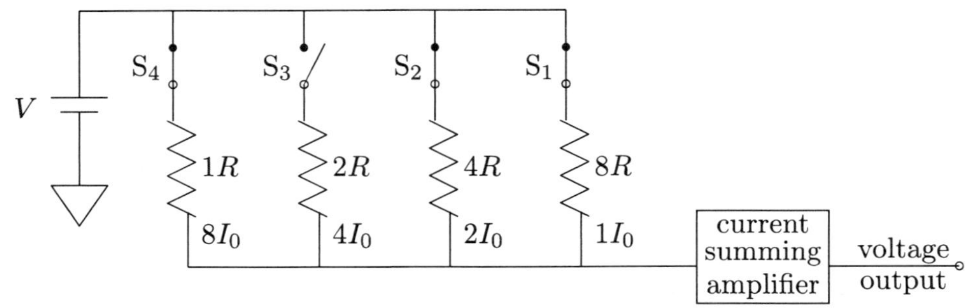

Figure 9.1: Binary weighted resister D/A converter. Here the switches are set to the binary code of 1011.

code is the current in analog signal. As an example, closing switches S_4, S_2, and S_1 represents binary number 1011 which is

$$1 \times 2^3 + 0 \times 2^2 + 1 \times 2^1 + 1 \times 2^0 = 11. \tag{9.1}$$

This type of D/A converter is easy to understand the mechanism. However, since the resistance in switch S_n is $1/2^{n-1}$ of the resistance in switch S_1, the range of resistances would be too large to be practical for the typical number of digital bits.

By arranging resistors cleverly, we can use only two sizes of resistors for the resistance ladder arrangement of D/A converter such as shown in Fig.9.2. The resolution of the analog signal is about half of the value of the least significant bit, i.e., about 2^{-n} times the full scale value of analog output voltage for n-bit D/A converter.

- A/D Converter ; Convert an analog signal from experimental device to a digital signal for computer.

A 4-bit A/D converter for analog signal of 0 to 10 V has the binary

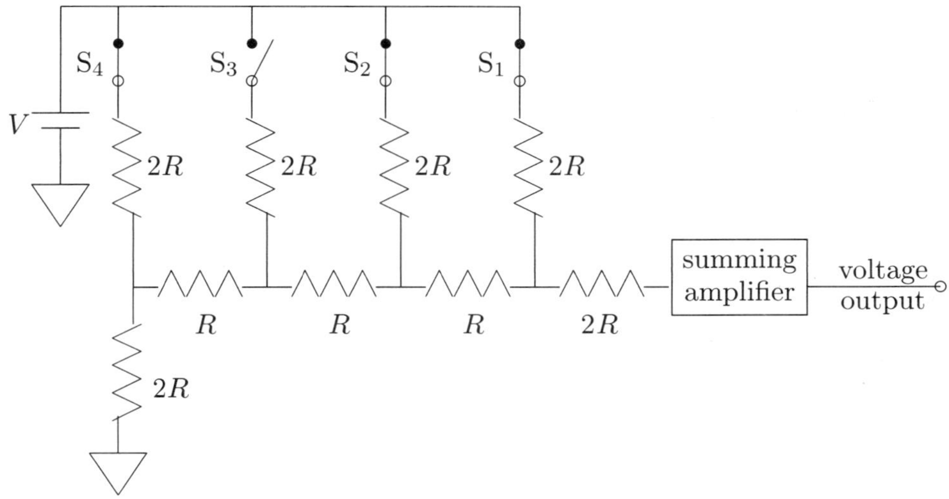

Figure 9.2: R–$2R$ network D/A converter. Here the switches are set to the binary code of 1011.

representation of

binary code	voltage	decimal value
1111	10.000 V	$2^4 - 1 = 15$
1000	5.333 V	$2^3 = 8$
0100	2.667 V	$2^2 = 4$
0010	1.333 V	$2^1 = 2$
0001	0.667 V	$2^0 = 1$
0000	0.000 V	0

To convert analog signal (7.50 V as an example) using 4-bit A/D converter as shown in Fig.9.3, compare the input analog signal with the signal converted from a digital signal in storage register. The converter consisted with a 4-bit storage register to store digitalized binary code, 4-bit D/A converter to convert binary code in the storage register, comparator to compare input analog signal with the signal converted from binary code, and programmer parts to perform comparison successively. Starting at the left-most (most significant) bit of storage

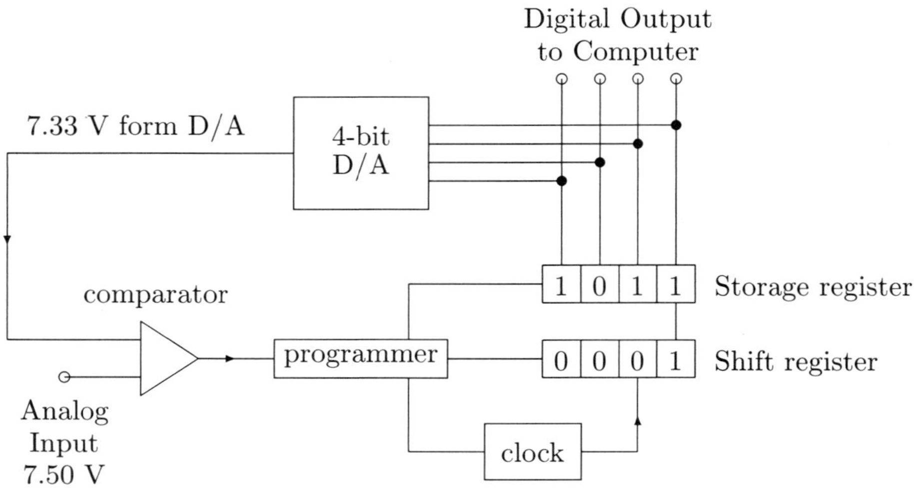

Figure 9.3: 4-bit A/D converter. The A/D converter shown here is in the state it would be at the time when the last bit is tested.

register turned on:

1. Try binary code 1000 in storage register which is converted to 5.333 V by D/A converter. Since the analog signal 7.50 V is larger than 5.333 V, keep the most significant bit turned on.
2. Try binary code 1100 which is 8.000 V. Since the input signal 7.50 V is smaller than 8.000 V, turn off the second significant bit thus the storage register is 1000.
3. Try binary code 1010 which is 6.667 V. Since 7.50 V is larger than 6.667 V, keep the third significant bit turned on thus binary code is 1010.
4. Try binary code 1011 in storage register which is 7.333 V. Since 7.50 V is larger than 7.333 V, keep the fourth bit turned on thus the binary code is 1011.
5. The final binary code 1011 is the digital output of A/D converter representing the analog signal of 7.500 V in a 4-bit A/D converter.

The precision of n-bit A/D converter is one part in 2^n of full range. For a 10 V input signal in 4-bit A/D converter, the precision would be ± 0.625 V.

- Amplification and Noise ; Transmit signal effectively between computer and experimental equipment.

  Signal with a larger amplitude has a larger signal to noise ratio and thus has less affection from noise. A digital signal is less affective by the noise than an analog signal. Thus it is better to put the A/D converter and the D/A converter at the site of experimental equipment than at the computer site.

Chapter 10

Data Analysis

10.1 Mean Value and Standard Deviation

Measured value in experiment is usually different from the real value of the physical quantity. The accuracy of measured value depends on measuring device, environment, human error, etc.

Error: difference between a measured value and the real value.
Relative error: ratio of the error to the real value.

Source of systematic error:

- Measuring device; scale, accuracy ...
- Environment of measurement; temperature, pressure, humidity ...
- Habit of person.
- Theoretical relation between variables of measurement.

The systematic error can be reduced by careful measurement using more accurate measuring device in well controlled environment. Systematic error can also be compensated after measurement.

Source of random error:

- Small variation of environment.

- Thickness of scale tick mark.
- Small change of human factor.

The random error has no control.
Characteristics of random error in repeated many measurements:

1. The probability occurring negative error is same as the probability of positive error with the same magnitude.
2. The probability of occurring small error is larger than the probability of larger error.
3. The probability occurring a very large error (order of the smallest scale of measuring device) is very small.

Thus if we repeat measurement infinitely many times, then the most probable measured value would be closest to the real value.

According to the characteristics 1 and 2 of random error, for the real value X, the sum of errors of the N measured values x_i is zero if the number of measurement N is infinitely large.

$$\sum_{i=1}^{\infty}(x_i - X) = 0 \implies X = \lim_{N\to\infty} \frac{1}{N}\sum_{i=1}^{N} x_i$$

For a large but finite N,

$$\sum_{i=1}^{\infty}(x_i - X) \approx \sum_{i=1}^{N}(x_i - x_0) = 0 \implies x_0 = \frac{1}{N}\sum_{i=1}^{N} x_i \qquad (10.1)$$

Thus the arithmetic mean value x_0 approaches to the real value X as the number of measurements N becomes larger and larger. On the other hand, according to the characteristics 2 and 3 of random error, as the measured values (data) x_i distribute more sharply around the real value X, the standard deviation σ of the data

$$\sigma^2 = \frac{1}{N}\sum_{i=1}^{N}(x_i - X)^2 \qquad (10.2)$$

is smaller. The standard deviation of data σ is independent of the number of measurements N if N is not too small. This σ does not represent the reliability of the mean value x_0 to be close to the actual value X. It just represents how sharply the data is distributed.

For the reliability of the mean value x_0, we define the standard deviation of mean value σ_0 as the magnitude of difference between the mean value of data and the real value,

$$\begin{aligned}\sigma_0^2 &= |x_0 - X|^2 = \left[\frac{1}{N}\sum_{i=1}^{N} x_i - X\right]^2 \\ &= \frac{1}{N^2}\left[\sum_i (x_i - X)^2 + \sum_{i\neq j}(x_i - X)(x_j - X)\right] \\ &= \frac{1}{N^2}\sum_{i=1}^{N}(x_i - X)^2 = \frac{1}{N}\sigma^2. \qquad (10.3)\end{aligned}$$

The second term in the second line vanished due to the characteristic 1 of random error. Smaller value of the standard deviation of the mean value σ_0 means higher reliability of the mean value x_0 to be close to the actual value X. Thus the reliability of the mean value x_0 becomes better as the number of measurements N becomes larger as $1/\sqrt{N}$.

Since we do not know the real value X we cannot use Eq.(10.2). However we know the mean value x_0. Using Eqs.(10.1) – (10.3),

$$\begin{aligned}N\sigma^2 &= \sum_{i=1}^{N}(x_i - X)^2 = \sum_i (x_i - x_0 + x_0 - X)^2 \\ &= \sum_i (x_i - x_0)^2 + \sum_i (x_0 - X)^2 = \sum_i (x_i - x_0)^2 + \sigma^2. \qquad (10.4)\end{aligned}$$

Thus the standard deviation σ of the data and the standard deviation σ_0 of the mean value x_0 are

$$\sigma^2 = \frac{1}{(N-1)}\sum_{i=1}^{N}(x_i - x_0)^2, \qquad (10.5)$$

$$\sigma_0 = |x_0 - X| = \frac{\sigma}{\sqrt{N}} \qquad (10.6)$$

The standard deviation of data σ is independent of the number of measurements N for not too small N. It depends only on the distribution form of the measured data. But the standard deviation of the mean value σ_0 is proportional to $1/\sqrt{N}$. Thus the reliability of the mean value is better for larger number of measurements. Finally, the measured value for X is $x_0 \pm \sigma_0$.

10.2 Chi-Square Fitting and Error Analysis

For an experimental value which are measured directly, the arithmetic mean value given by Eq.(10.1) is good for the mean value of data which replaces the real value X. For a physical quantity which is not determined by direct measurement but determined through a relation with some other directly measured quantities, the simple arithmetic mean value cannot represents the real value X. For a physical quantity which can be measured directly, the arithmetic mean value of Eq.(10.1) can be looked as minimizing the standard deviation σ^2 of Eq.(10.2) (replaced the real value X by the mean value x_0) with respect to the mean value x_0, i.e.,

$$\frac{d}{dx_0}\left[\sum_{i=1}^{N}(x_i - x_0)^2\right] = 2\sum_{i=1}^{N}(x_i - x_0) = 0. \tag{10.7}$$

This is the least chi square method for mean value of directly measured data.

Various physical quantities are connected through a relation according to the physical law of the phenomena. For indirectly measurable variables a, b, c, ... and directly measurable variables x, y, z, ..., a functional relation

$$f(x, y, z, \cdots; a, b, c, \cdots) = 0 \tag{10.8}$$

represents the law of the underlying physical phenomena. As an example, Ohm's law is $f(V, I; R) = V - RI = 0$ for determining resistance R by measuring voltage V and current I. For N sets of directly measured values $\{x_i, y_i, z_i, \ldots\}$, the value of $f_i = f(x_i, y_i, z_i, \cdots; a, b, c, \cdots)$ may not be zero exactly due to the error of measurement. The systematic error of f_i can be controlled but the random error of f_i has the same characteristics as the random error of direct measurement. Thus the chi square is defined as the weighted sum of squared error f_i^2

$$\chi^2 = \sum_{i=1}^{N} w_i f_i^2 = \sum_{i=1}^{N} w_i \left| f(x_i, y_i, z_i, \cdots; a, b, c, \cdots)\right|^2 \tag{10.9}$$

where the weight w_i represents the reliability of the data set $\{x_i, y_i, z_i, \ldots\}$. The chi square per data is χ^2/N. The least chi square fitting method (최소제곱법) determines the values of a, b, c, ... by minimizing the chi square. Through the weight factor w_i in the χ^2, the evaluated values $\{a, b, c, \cdots\}$ are fitted to give smaller error of $|f_i|$ for the more reliably measured value set with larger weight w_i than the less reliable data set with smaller weight w_i. If a systematic error σ_i varies for data set by set then the weight factor can be set to $w_i = \sigma_i^{-2}$. Eq.(10.7) for direct measurements corresponds to the case of least chi square fitting for $a = X$ with $w_i = 1$, i.e., with a non-varying systematic error ($\sigma_i = \sigma$).

As an example, for the case of determining resistance R through Ohm's law, $V = RI$,

$$\chi^2 = \sum_{i=1}^{N} |f(V_i, I_i; R)|^2 = \sum_{i=1}^{N} (V_i - RI_i)^2, \tag{10.10}$$

$$\frac{\partial \chi^2}{\partial R} = 2\sum_{i=1}^{N} (V_i - RI_i)I_i = 0 \implies R = \frac{\left[\sum_i V_i I_i\right]/N}{\left[\sum_i I_i^2\right]/N} \tag{10.11}$$

Here the resistance R is given as the ratio of the arithmetic mean of power $\overline{VI}$ to the arithmetic mean of current square $\overline{I^2}$. On the other hand, if we use the form of $f(V, I; R) = R - V/I$ for the Ohm's law, then we have

$$\chi^2 = \sum_{i=1}^{N} \left(R - \frac{V_i}{I_i}\right)^2 = \sum_{i=1}^{N} \frac{1}{I_i^2} (V_i - RI_i)^2, \tag{10.12}$$

$$\frac{\partial \chi^2}{\partial R} = 2\sum_{i=1}^{N} \left(R - \frac{V_i}{I_i}\right) = 0 \implies R = \frac{1}{N}\sum_{i=1}^{N} \left[\frac{V_i}{I_i}\right] \tag{10.13}$$

Now the resistance R is the arithmetic mean $\overline{V/I}$ of resistance $R_i = V_i/I_i$ for each measurement. The Eq.(10.12) is different from the Eq.(10.10) by the factor of I_i^{-2}. In Eq.(10.10), every data set $\{V_i, I_i\}$ are treated with the same weight $w_i = 1$ while each data set $\{V_i, I_i\}$ are weighted with $w_i = I_i^{-2}$, i.e., the smaller current has larger weight in Eq.(10.12). The Eq.(10.12) corresponds to giving a same weight to the data $R_i = V_i/I_i$ rather than to the data set $\{V_i, I_i\}$. If one set of voltmeter and ammeter is used for whole data sets then Eq.(10.10) would be more proper.

As another example, consider measurement of the resistivity ρ of metal at various temperature T (assume here that both ρ and T are measured directly). From these directly measured data sets, we extract two physical quantities of temperature coefficient α of resistivity and the resistivity ρ_0 at temperature T_0. The resistivity ρ and the temperature T are related by

$$f(\rho, T; \rho_0, \alpha) = \rho_0[1 + \alpha(T - T_0)] - \rho = 0. \tag{10.14}$$

The chi square fitting becomes, with $\beta = \rho_0\alpha$,

$$\begin{aligned}
\chi^2 &= \sum_{i=1}^{N} [\rho_0 + \beta(T_i - T_0) - \rho_i]^2, \\
\frac{\partial \chi^2}{\partial \rho_0} &= 2\sum_{i=1}^{N} [(\rho_0 - \rho_i) + \beta(T_i - T_0)] = 0, \\
\frac{\partial \chi^2}{\partial \beta} &= 2\sum_{i=1}^{N} [(\rho_0 - \rho_i) + \beta(T_i - T_0)]\,(T_i - T_0) = 0.
\end{aligned} \tag{10.15}$$

From these coupled equations for ρ_0 and $\beta = \alpha\rho_0$,

$$\begin{aligned}
\rho_0 &= \frac{[\sum_i \rho_i/N]\,[\sum_i (T_i - T_0)^2/N] - [\sum_i (T_i - T_0)/N]\,[\sum_i \rho_i (T_i - T_0)/N]}{[\sum_i (T_i - T_0)^2/N] - [\sum_i (T_i - T_0)/N]^2} \\
\beta &= \frac{[\sum_i \rho_i (T_i - T_0)/N] - [\sum_i \rho_i/N]\,[\sum_i (T_i - T_0)/N]}{[\sum_i (T_i - T_0)^2/N] - [\sum_i (T_i - T_0)/N]^2} \\
\alpha &= \frac{[\sum_i \rho_i (T_i - T_0)/N] - [\sum_i \rho_i/N]\,[\sum_i (T_i - T_0)/N]}{[\sum_i \rho_i/N]\,[\sum_i (T_i - T_0)^2/N] - [\sum_i (T_i - T_0)/N]\,[\sum_i \rho_i (T_i - T_0)/N]}
\end{aligned} \tag{10.16}$$

Here β is used instead of α itself in minimizing χ^2 since ρ_0 and β form a set of coupled linear equations.

Finally, consider the case of determining the time constant $\tau = RC$ of an R-C circuit. The voltage across the capacitor during the charging process with emf of E is $V(t) = E(1 - e^{-t/\tau})$ which can be represented either by

$$f(V, t; \tau) = V - E(1 - e^{-t/\tau}) = 0 \tag{10.17}$$

or by

$$f(V, t; \tau) = t + \tau \ln\left(1 - \frac{V}{E}\right) = 0. \tag{10.18}$$

with the directly measured data sets of $\{V_i, t_i\}$. Since the time t appears in the exponent, for the case of Eq.(10.17), the chi square has a larger weight for the data set measured at smaller time than the data set at larger time. In contrast to this, the time t appears linear for the case of Eq.(10.18) and all the measured data sets have the same weight. However more importantly, the form of Eq.(10.18) is much easier in extracting the value of the time constant τ using least χ^2 fitting than the form of Eq.(10.17) since τ appears linearly in Eq.(10.18) while τ appears exponentially in Eq.(10.17). If we can make $f(x, y, z, \cdots; a, b, c, \cdots)$ linear in the variables a, b, c, $\cdots$ which should be determined by chi square fitting, it is better using linear form of f than using nonlinear form unless the reliability of data set requires otherwise.

For the reliability of mean values of the indirectly measured quantities $\{a, b, c, \cdots\}$, we can define the standard deviation for each mean value a_0, b_0, c_0, $\cdots$ in the same way as the standard deviation Eq.(10.6) of a directly measured quantity. That is, for the standard deviation of mean value of quantity a,

$$\sigma_a^2 = |a_0 - a|^2 = \frac{1}{N}\left[\frac{1}{(N-1)}\sum_{i=1}^{N}(a_i - a_0)^2\right] \tag{10.19}$$

Through the functional relation f, the deviations of data a_i, b_i, c_i, $\cdots$ from their corresponding mean values a_0, b_0, c_0, $\cdots$ are related with the deviation of directly measured data x_i, x_i, z_i, $\cdots$ from their mean values x_0, y_0, z_0, $\cdots$;

$$\begin{aligned} df &= \left(\frac{\partial f}{\partial a}\right) da + \left(\frac{\partial f}{\partial b}\right) db + \left(\frac{\partial f}{\partial c}\right) dc + \cdots \\ &\quad + \left(\frac{\partial f}{\partial x}\right) dx + \left(\frac{\partial f}{\partial y}\right) dy + \left(\frac{\partial f}{\partial z}\right) dz + \cdots \end{aligned} \tag{10.20}$$

The deviation $da_i = a_i - a_0$ of a_i from its mean value a_0 is then, with $db_i = 0$, $dc_i = 0$, $\cdots$

$$da_i = -\left(\frac{\partial f}{\partial a}\right)^{-1}\left[\left(\frac{\partial f}{\partial x}\right) dx_i + \left(\frac{\partial f}{\partial y}\right) dy_i + \left(\frac{\partial f}{\partial z}\right) dz_i + \cdots\right]$$

where $dx_i = x_i - x_0$, $dy_i = y_i - y_0$, and $dz_i = z_i - z_0$. Thus the standard deviation of the mean value a_0 is

$$\sigma_a^2 = \left(\frac{\partial f}{\partial a}\right)^{-2}\left[\left(\frac{\partial f}{\partial x}\right)^2 \sigma_x^2 + \left(\frac{\partial f}{\partial y}\right)^2 \sigma_y^2 + \left(\frac{\partial f}{\partial z}\right)^2 \sigma_z^2 + \cdots\right] \tag{10.21}$$

The standard deviation of mean values b_0, c_0, $\cdots$ are similarly given. Thus once we find the standard deviation σ_x, σ_y, σ_z, $\cdots$ of mean values x_0, y_0, z_0, $\cdots$ for the directly measured quantities, then we can find the standard deviation σ_a, σ_b, σ_c, $\cdots$ of mean values a_0, b_0, c_0, $\cdots$ for the indirectly measured quantities for their reliability.

Some data has a form of linear superposition of special functions of some variables as parameter;

$$y(x) = C_1 g_1(x) + C_2 g_2(x) + C_3 g_3(x) + \cdots \tag{10.22}$$

where $g_1(x)$, $g_2(x)$, $g_3(x)$, $\cdots$ are known functions of parameter x. For this case, the coefficients C_1, C_2, C_3, $\cdots$ can be determined from the measured data sets of $\{x_i, y_i\}$ using the least chi square fitting with

$$f(x, y; C_1, C_2, C_3, \cdots) = y(x) - [C_1 g_1(x) + C_2 g_2(x) + C_3 g_3(x) + \cdots] .$$

The reliability of the mean value of the coefficients can be obtained in terms of the standard deviation of directly measured x and y through Eq.(10.21). Expanding angular distribution in terms of Legendre polynomial is an example of this method. Fourier series expansion or wavelet analysis can also be considered as expanding in terms of special functions using chi square fitting.

10.3 Fast Fourier Transform (FFT)

If the functions $g_l(x)$ in Eq.(10.22) are orthonormalized functions, i.e.,

$$\int_0^L g_l^*(x) g_{l'}(x) dx = \delta_{ll'} \tag{10.23}$$

then the expansion coefficients C_l can be obtained by

$$C_l = \int_0^L g_l^*(x) y(x) dx = \frac{L}{N} \sum_{i=1}^{N} g_l^*(x_i) y_i \tag{10.24}$$

from the measured data sets $\{x_i, y_i\}$.

One such example is the Fourier series expansion of a periodic function $y(x)$ with period L:

$$y(x) = \frac{1}{2}A_0 + \sum_{n=1}^{\infty}\left[A_n \cos(nk_0x) + B_n \sin(nk_0x)\right], \qquad (10.25)$$

$$A_n = \frac{2}{L}\int_{x_0-L/2}^{x_0+L/2} y(x)\cos(nk_0x)dx, \qquad (10.26)$$

$$B_n = \frac{2}{L}\int_{x_0-L/2}^{x_0+L/2} y(x)\sin(nk_0x)dx \qquad (10.27)$$

where $k_0 = 2\pi/L$. Since $e^{ix} = \cos x + i\sin x$, Fourier series expansion can also be represented as

$$y(x) = \sum_{n=-\infty}^{\infty} C_n e^{ink_0x}, \qquad (10.28)$$

$$C_n = \frac{1}{L}\int_{x_0-L/2}^{x_0+L/2} y(x)e^{-ink_0x}dx, \qquad (10.29)$$

$$A_n = C_n + C_{-n} \quad \text{and} \quad B_n = i(C_n - C_{-n}). \qquad (10.30)$$

For $L \to \infty$, Eq.(10.28) becomes Fourier integral,

$$y(x) = \frac{1}{\sqrt{2\pi}}\int_{-\infty}^{\infty} \eta(k)e^{ikx}dk, \qquad (10.31)$$

$$\eta(k) = \frac{1}{\sqrt{2\pi}}\int_{-\infty}^{\infty} y(x)e^{-ikx}dx. \qquad (10.32)$$

This is called Fourier transformation.

Fast Fourier transform (FFT) is a computational algorithm to make fast the Fourier transform in discretized $x_j = (j-1)\Delta$ space (data sets of $\{x_j, y_j\}$). As an example, using Eq.(10.29) for Fourier series of Eq.(10.28),

$$C_n = \frac{1}{N}\sum_{j=1}^{N} y_j e^{-ink_0x_j} = \frac{\Delta}{L}\sum_{j=1}^{N} y_j \left(e^{-ik_0\Delta}\right)^{(j-1)n} = \frac{\Delta}{L}w^{-n}F_n. \qquad (10.33)$$

In the second form $w = e^{-ik_0\Delta}$ is calculated once and only the simple multiplication of w^{jn} is needed for each term of $F_n = \sum_j y_j w^{jn}$. The number of multiplications of w for w^{jn} in each term is N^2. For even N,

$$F_n = \sum_{j=1}^{N/2} w^{(2j-1)n} y_{2j-1} + w^n \sum_{j=1}^{N/2} w^{2jn} y_{2j} = F_n^o + w^n F_n^e. \qquad (10.34)$$

Since only $N/2$ terms appear in each of F_n^o and F_n^e with multiplication of w^2, the number of multiplication of w^2 for each of these is $(N/2)^2$ and thus $N^2/2$ in total. If N is a power of 2, this reduction can be done for $\log_2 N$ steps and reduces the number of multiplication w can be reduced to be order of N.

10.4 Wavelet Analysis

Fourier series expansion is good only for a periodic function which repeats a same form of function for infinitely many times. Thus we can expand in terms of trigonometric functions which oscillate for infinite number of periods. For the case of function with a form of many localized functions superposed, such as heart beat signal or superposition of many Gaussian functions, we expand using wavelet which corresponds to a wave function in a short range of the parameter variable x. In a wavelet analysis for heart beat, the position and amplitude of the wavelet representing the basic form of heart beat can be extracted from the data. For the case of superposed Gaussians, the amplitude A_i, the position x_i, and the width σ_i of the Gaussian function

$$G_i(x) = A_i e^{-(x-x_i)^2/(2\sigma_i^2)} \tag{10.35}$$

can be extracted in a wavelet analysis. The least chi square method can be used in wavelet analysis.

Chapter 11

Text Editing and Graphics for Reports

To publish any result, a manuscript should be edited with tables and figures. Editing programs and graphic packages have two types. One is interactive WYSIWYG (What You See Is What You Get) type in which you can see the final result while you create the file. In non-interactive type, you cannot see the final result when you create the file. The final result can be seen only after compiling the created file. However it is easier to change the contents of the file than WYSIWYG type.

11.1 Graphics

- Interactive Graphics : Excel, Axum ...
- Non-interactive Graphics : PGPLOT (use Fortran language),
Mathematica, ...
- Graph Out File : Post Script (Encapsulated PS) file, pdf, bit map file,
GIF, JPG ....

11.2 Text Editing Program

- Ascii Editor : vi editor in Unix, DOS editor, Notepad, Wordpad ...
  For a simple text form only without equation, figure, etc.

- Interactive : HWP (아래아한글), MS-word, ..
  When add or remove any of equation, table, figure, or reference, the number of them should be corrected by hand everywhere.

- Non-interactive : Tex, LaTeX, Revtex, KpsTex (See Appendix E)
  The numbering of equation, figure, table, reference, or page are automatically done by the LaTeX program. When any equation or table, figure are added or removed, the adjusted new numbers are assigned and they are referred correctly in text by compiling the LaTeX file.

11.3 Presentation

To present result in oral, view graph should be created.

- Interactive : ppt (power point), ...

- Non-interactive : SLiTeX (LaTeX)

Appendix A

Unix Commands

Basic commands for Unix or Linux operating system. The same commands using in Linux, DOS or VMS operating system are shown after colon.

Unix Commands

logout or exit
    logout from unix host and disconnect
ls : dir
    list file and directory name
    ls -l ; list in long form, detailed information
    ls -l | more ; list files screen by screen
man : help
    help for commands
    man command
passwd
    change password
pwd
    show present working directory
mkdir : md
    make subdirectory
rmdir
    remove directory
cd

change directory

cd . ; present directory,

cd .. ; one level above,

cd ~ ; home directory,

cd / ; root directory

rm : del

delete file

cp : copy

cp filefrom fileto

mv : move, rename

move filefrom fileto

more file : page

display file one full window at a time; space bar for next screen

vi : edit

visual editor, full screen editor

see next page for the vi editor commands

lpr file.name : print

print a file named file.name (-Pprinterquename)

lpr -b file.name ; print a binary file named file.name

lpq or lpstat ; display status of jobs in print queue

mail

email read or send

elm, pine ...

telnet host.name

rlogin, host, ssh ...

ftp host.name

file transfer

fort77 or f77

compile and link fortran program

cc or g77

compile and link c program

ps

process status

jobs

display list of processes (jobs)

kill nn

kill process number nn

chmod

change access mode for owner, group, others (chmod 755 for webpage)

users

who

which

whatis

whereis

sh

batch

execute a batch script file

CNTRL d ; make batch job to a background job and go back to unix command mode

CNTRL c

kill current job

CNTRL z : Do not use this

Put current processor to background job which remains in the system even after log off. If used this by mistake, then use fg to bring it up

fg

Bring any job in background back up

CNTRL s

stop (freeze) the screen

CNTRL q

release screen which stopped by CNTRL s

vi editor commands

At Full Screen Command Mode

arrows (or h, j, k, l) ; move the cursor to the direction of arrow

CNTRL f ; move down one page forward

CNTRL b ; move up one page backward

CNTRL g ; give the current position of the cursor (line number and column number)

nnG ; go to the nn-th line from top

G ; go to the end of file

0 (zero) ; go to the beginning of the current line

$; go to the end of the current line
/word ; search forward for occurrence of the word
?word ; search backward for occurrence of the word
n ; search next occurrence of the previous search word
N ; search next occurrence but in reversed direction
x ; delete a character at the cursor position
s ; substitute a character at the cursor position, then go to insert mode
S ; substitute a line at the cursor position; delete and go to insert mode
dd ; delete a line at the cursor position
i ; go to insert mode
ESC key or CNTRL c ; go back from insert mode to command mode
: ; go to command line

At Command Line

nn ; go to the line number nn
d ; delete the line at the cursor position
dnn ; delete nn lines from the cursor position
dw ; delete up to the beginning of the next word
db ; delete up to the previous word
n1,n2 d ; delete lines from the line number n1 to the line number n2
J ; join the line with cursor and the next line into one line
n1,n2 m n3 ; move lines n1 through n2 after line n3
n1,n2 co n3 ; copy lines n1 through n2 after line n3
n1,n2 s/string1/string2/cg ; substitute string1 by string2 occurring in lines n1 - n2 (every one (g) by confirming (c))
r file.name ; read in the file named file.name and insert at the cursor position
w ; save (write) any changes made
q ; quit the vi editor when there was no change after previous saving
q! ; quit vi editor neglecting any changes made in the session
wq ; save any changes made and then quit the vi editor
help ; help for vi editor commands

Appendix B

HTML Commands

The structure and basic commands of HTML, Hyper Text Markup Language.

Basic structure of HTML file (문서 기본형식)

<HTML>
<HEAD>
<TITLE> Name of Web page </TITLE>
<BASE TARGET="second_window">
    first_window, _blank, _self, _parent, _top
<LINK HREF="connection file or url" TITLE="title" REL="...">
    make link tool bar ; * for MOSAIC
<script language="javascript">
    define javascript functions
</script>
</HEAD>
<BODY>
<BODY BACKGROUND="file" BGCOLOR="color" TEXT="color" LINK="color" ALINK="color" VLINK="color">
    color : bbrrgg (000000 – ffffff), blue, red, green, yellow ...
    ALINK ; at link, VLINK ; linked before

..... Contents of document (내용부분) ......

</BODY>
</HTML>

For Body Part

<H*n* ALIGN="position"> Aligned Heading <H*n* >
<h1> ..... </h1> Largest
....
<h6> ..... </h6> Smallest
position : left, center, right
<FONT SIZE="size" COLOR="color" FACE="face">..text..</FONT>
size : 1 ~ 7 (small → large) (watch the order)
<BASEFONT SIZE="size"> set base font
Font Type Setting
<B> ..... **text in Bold Face** ..... </B>
<I> ..... *text in Italic Face* ..... </I>
<U> ..... Underlined text ..... </U>
<BLINK> ..... Blinking text ...... </BLINK>
<BIG> ..... text in Big Letters ..... <BIG>
<SMALL> ..... text in Small Letters ..... </SMALL>
_{..... Subscript text .....}
^{..... Superscript text .....}
Block Formatting

 : Break Line
<P ALIGN="center"> .... </P> : New Paragraph
(either <P> ... </P> or <P> ...)
<CENTER> .... </CENTER> : Center line (LEFT, RIGHT)
<ALIGN="center"> (left, right)
<PRE> ...... </PRE> : Presetted format by text
<CITE> ..... </CITE> : Citation
<EM> ...... </EM> : Emphasize
<STRONG> ..... </STRONG> : Emphasize
<SAMP> ..... </SAMP> : Sample
<!– .... –> : Comments
<HR ALIGN="....." NOSHADE SIZE="...." WIDTH="....">
horizontal line

<A HREF=Destination Options> Destination indicator </A>
Connect to other Site or File
Destination : /path/file_name, URL, or #MoveTo
URL : Uniform Resolution Locator
HTTP://host.name/path/file.name
HTTPS://secured.host.name
TELNET://host.name
FTP://host.name/directory
MAILTO:userid@host.name
GOPHER://gopher.host.name
#MoveTo
move to the line having <A NAME=MoveTo>Position Name</A>
Options
TARGET="target", TITLE="title"
<IMG SRC=source Options> Image Name </IMG>
ALIGN= TOP, MIDDLE, BOTTOM, LEFT, RIGHT
WIDTH= HEIGHT= nn (pixels) or nn% (percent of window size)
VSPACE= HSPACE= nn (pixels)
BORDER=nn : border line thickness nn pixels
ALT="texts" : texts to show when Image is not shown
<SOUND SRC=source Options>
LOOP="number of loops" : INFINITE or -1
DELAY="delay time (in seconds)"
List
<OL TYPE=.... START="no"> ...... </OL> : Ordered List
TYPE= Default(arabic), I, i, A, a
<UL TYPE=.....> .... </UL> : Unordered List
TYPE= DISK(default), CIRCLE, SQUARE
<LI VALUE="no"> texts : item of list
<DL> ...... </DL> : Definition List
<DT> title text : Definition Title
<DD> defining texts : Explanation texts to define Definition Title
Table
<TABLE options><tr> ...... </tr></TABLE>
BORDER, ALIGN, WIDTH, HEIGHT, CELLSPACING,
CELLPADING, FRAME, RULES

<TR ALIGN="....." VALIGN="....."><td> ...... </td></TR>
<TD ROWSPAN=rows COLSPAN=columns ALIGN=... VALIGN=..>
Elements </TD>
<table><tr><td> ..... Elements ..... </td></tr></table>

<FRAMESET ROWS="..." COLS="..." FRAMEBORDER="yes"
BORDER="1">
<FRAME SRC="menu1.html" NAME="menu1" Options>
<FRAME SRC="menu2.html" NAME="menu2" Options>
</FRAMESET>
<NOFRAME> no frame </NOFRAME>
ROWS="100, 50%, *, 10%" : Height of each row
100 pixels, 50% of total height, remaining height, 10% height
COLS="100, 30%, *, 20%" - : Width of each column
100 pixels, 30% of total width, remaining width, 20% width
FRAMEBORDER="yes or no" or "1 or 0" : frame border line
BORDER="nn" : border size number
SRC="menu.html" : html file for this frame
NAME="frame-name" : name of the frame
MARGINWIDTH="nn" : width of left, right margin in pixels
MARGINHEIGHT="nn" : height of top, bottom margin in pixels
SCROLLING="yes, no, or auto" : scroll bar in frame
NORESIZE : prevent resizing of frame with mouse

Escape sequence for Special Characters : in &...: form
< : <
> : >
≤ : ≤
≥ : ≥
& : &
" : "
  : blank

Mathematical Equation
$.........$
∫ ∞, &sin; &tanh;, α ......
<box> ...... </box> : ......
_{......}, ^{......}

<over> : Fractional
<above> ...... </above>, <below> ...... </below>
<vec>, <bar>, <dot>, <ddot>, <hat>, <tilde>
<sqrt> ..... </sqrt>, <root> ..... </root>, <array> ..... </array>
<text> ..... </text>, <b>, <t>, <bt>

Some Physics Related Sites

- physics.khu.ac.kr or physics.kyunghee.ac.kr : 응용물리학과 (Dept. of Applied Physics, Kyung Hee University)
- www.khu.ac.kr or www.kyunghee.ac.kr : 경희대학교 (Kyung Hee University)
- xxx.lanl.gov : preprint depository site
- www.kps.or.kr : 한국물리학회 (Korean Physical Society)
- icpr.snu.ac.kr : 물리전문연구정보센터 (Information Center for Physics Research)
- www.aps.org : American Physical Society (미국물리학회)
  publish.aps.org : APS Journal (미국물리학회 학술지)
- www.elsevier.nl ; Elsevier 학술지 출판소
  https://ppp.elsevier.nl : Nuclear Physics Publishing Process
- Common form of Web Site Address :
  www.organizationname.organizationtype.country,
  home.···, info.···, physics.···, phys.···, phys1.···, computername.···,

Appendix C

Fortran Commands

Basic commands for Fortran language. The same commands using in C language are shown after colon.

type name_list
  REAL*4,REAL*8,REAL, COMPLEX*16, CHARACTER*n,
  LOGICAL, IMPLICIT type [implicit real*8 (a-h, o-z)]
PARAMETER (name=value) : #define name value
COMMON /name/ list
DIMENSION list : array
  array(nd1,nd2,nd3,...) : a11,a21,a31,...,a12,a22,a32,...,a13,a23,a33,......
EQUIVALENCE (name1,name2,...) : union
EXTERNAL Routine_name
  use name of subroutine or function routine itself as parameter
  INTRINSIC
C or * at column 1 : /*.......*/
  column 1 ; comment line if c or *
  column 1 – 5 ; label
  column 6 ; continuation
  column 7 – 72 ; Fortran Statements
  column 73 – 80 ; comments
  ! ; start comments
DATA name /value/ or /(value1, value2 ...)/

Statement

```
    Variable = Expression
    (+, -), (*, /), **, (....)
GOTO
        GO TO nnn
        GO TO (n1, n2, n3 ..., nk) intvl (positive)
    nnn CONTINUE or Statement ; c1-c5, c7-c72
IF
    IF(Conditional Expression) Statement
    IF(Conditional Expression) THEN
        Statements
        ENDIF
    IF(Conditional Expression) THEN
        Statements1
        ELSE
        Statements2
        ENDIF
    IF(Expr1) THEN
        .......
        ELSE IF(Expr2) THEN
        .......
        ELSE
        ......
        ENDIF
    * (.EQ., .LT., .GT., .GE.), .NOT., .AND., .OR.
         (.XOR., .EQV., .NEQV.)
    IF(Expres) n1, n2, n3
DO ..... CONTINUE
        DO nnn iv = istrt, iend, istep
        ..........
        DO nnn jv = jstrt, jend, jstep
        ..........
    nnn CONTINUE
        Implied DO
            PRINT *, (AA(i), i=istrt,iend,istep)
        DO nnn WHILE(Expression)
        .............
```

```
    nnn END DO
READ (unit 5) : scanf
    READ *, aa, ab(5), (ia(i),i=1,3)
    READ fmtno, xx, xy
    READ(unit, fmt, ERR=nerr, END=nend) x, y
WRITE (unit 6) : printf
    PRINT *, aa, ab(5), (ia(i),i=1,3)
    PRINT fmtno, xx, yy
    WRITE(unit, fmt, ERR=nerr, END=nend) x, y
FORMAT
    fmtno FORMAT(fmt1, fmt2, fmt3 ......, fmtn) ; c1 – c5, c7 – c72
    wX ; skip w blank spaces
    Tn ; tap move to n-th column
    wHstring ; character string of length w
    [r]Aw ; r strings of width w
    [r]Lw ; r Logicals of width w (true or false according to first character,
            t or f)
    [r]Iw ; r integers of width w
    [r]Fw.d ; r reals of width w and decimals d
    [r]Ew.d ; r reals of width w and decimals d in form of xxx.ddd.Eee
    [r]Dw.d ; r double precisions in xxx.dddDee
    [r]Gw.d ; in either Fw.d or Ew.d form depending on the value of real
    nPfedg
    rZw ; r Hexadecimal number of width w
    / ; go to new line
    'string' ;
    r(fmt1, fmt2 ...) ; repeat (.....) r times
    For output (in first column of each line of output)
        ' ' ; new line
        '0' ; skip a line
        '1' ; new page
        '+' ; same line
        '-' ; skip two lines
STOP
    STOP "Normal Termination"
END
```

SUBROUTINE

```
PROGRAM prognam
SUBROUTINE subnam(para1, para2 ....., paran)
type FUNCTION funcnam(para1, para2 ....., paran)
ENTRY
RETURN
END
fncname(dat1, dat2 ....., datn) = expression
CALL subnam(para1, para2 ....., paran)
xx = yy + funcnam(para1, para2 ....., paran)
```

Intrinsic Library Functions

```
SIN(x) ; x in radian
COS(x)
TAN(x)
ATAN(x)
EXP(x)
ABS(x)
SQRT(x)
ALOG10(x)
ALOG(x)
FLOAT(i)
IFIX(x)
MOD(i1,i2)
CMPLX(r1,r2)
REAL(cx)
IMAG(cx)
CONJG(cx)
RAN(ii)
```

File Usage

```
OPEN([unit=]nu [, FILE='filename', IOSTAT=ios, STATUS='statu',
        RECL=lrecl, ACCESS='acces',FORM='formun', ERR=nn ])
statu ; OLD, NEW, SCRATCH, UNKNOWN
acces ; SEQUENTIAL, DIRECT
formun ; FORMATTED, UNFORMATTED
```

lrecl ; record length (in bytes)
CLOSE([unit=]nn [, ERR=nn, IOSTAT=ios])
stat ; KEEP, DELETE
REWIND([unit=]nn [, ERR=nn, IOSTAT=ios])

Compile and Link ; fort77 -o filexec -l library filename.f (f77)

Appendix D

C Commands

Basic commands for C language. The same commands using in Fortran language are shown after colon.

/* ..... comments ...... */
Preprocessors

    #include filename : #include <stdio.h>, #include "mylib.h"
    #define name[(parameters)] value-expression : PRAMETER
    #undef name
    if condition
    ..... statement ..... ;
    #elseif condition
    ..... statement ..... ;
    #else
    ..... statement ..... ;
    #endif
    #ifdef name : if name is defined
    ..... statement ..... ;
    #ifndef name : if name is not defined
    ..... statement ..... ;

Declaration of subroutine-function name (except int or void type)

    type sub1 (par1, par2)
    type sub2 (par.......)
    type sub3 (par.......)

Declaration of Global variables : COMMON Block

Integer : short, int, long, unsigned short, unsigned, unsigned long
Real : float, double, long double
Character : char, unsigned char, signed char
Enumerated : enum
    enum tagname elemnt1, elemnt2 ....., elemntn variablelist
Pointer : * &
    *p : p is pointer variable (value stored in address p)
    &var : pointer (address) of var
    Character string name or Array name is a pointer : do not use &
Structured : struct strctname item1; item2; ..... itemn; strctdatalist
    struct student long st_id; char age; float GPA; x, classa[30];
    x.st_id, x.age, classa[1].GPA
struct bitstrct bitfield1 : bitlnth1; ..... bitfieldn : bitlnthn
    bitwise structure
Shared : union : EQUIVALENCE
    union [unioname] char c; int i; float f; a;
    a.c, a.i, a.f
typeless : void
type array[n1][n2]....[nn]; : a[0][0], a[0][1], a[0][2] ....., a[0][n2-1], a[1][0],
    a[1][1], a[1][2] ....., a[1][n2-1], a[2][0] .....

main() or subname(para.....)
Routine Variables;
{ Block Variables; ..... }
Arithmetic Operators : (+ –) (* / %(MOD))
Relational Operators : (< <= > >=) (== !=)
Logical Operators : &&(and) ||(or) !(not)
Bitwise Operators : ˜(bitwise complement) &(bitwise AND)
    |(bitwise OR) ^ (bitwise XOR) <<(shift left) >>(shift right)
    (aa<>n; : shift aa by n bits)
= += –= *= /= %= <<= >>= &= ^= |=
    (a operator= c : a = a operator c)
Increment or decrement operator : ++ or – :
    x=1; y=x++; (y=1,x=2), y=++x; (y=2,x=2)
rslt = expr1 ? expr2 : expr3 : if(expr1) rslt=expr2; else rslt=expr3;
while (expression) {..... statements ......}
for (expr1;expr2; expr3) {..... statements ......} : DO nn i=i1,in,id

expr1; while (expr2) {..... statements ..... expr3;}
do {..... statements .....} while (exprs)
if(exprs) {..... statements .....}
if(exprs) {..... statem1 .....} else {..... statem2 .....}
switch(exprs) {case valu1 : statem1 break; case valu2 : statem2 break;
..... case valun : statemn break; default : statemd break;}
break
continue
goto label1; label1: statement;
sizeof(item) : in <stdlib.h>
sizeof : memory size of item in bytes
strlen : length of character string
strcpy : copy a character string
strcat : join two strings into one
strcmp : compare two character strings
strchr : position of a char in string
exit(n) : n=0 for normal termination
scanf("format", &item1, &item2 ......, &itemn)
printf("format", item1, item2 ......, itemn)
format : strings and %d %o %x %f %e %c %s %5d %7.4f %9.3e
* : skip
\0 : null character
\a : alert (bell)
\b : back space
\f : form feed
\n : new line
\r : carriage return
\t : horizontal tab
\v : vertical tab
\\ : back slash
\" : double quotation mark
\' : single quotation mark
\ : line continue
\nnn : octal
\more
type sub1 (par1, par2)

```
    { ......... ;
    ....... ; }
type sub2 (par.....)
    { ......... ;
    ....... ; return; }
type sub3 (par......)
    { ......... ;
    ....... ; return expression; }
Standard functions ()
    int getchar()    int putchar()
    char *gets(string)    char *puts(string)
    printf (fmt, par1, par2 ...)    scanf (fmt, par1, par2 ...)
    FILE *fopen(filename, filemode)
    int fclose(unitname)
    int getc()    int putc()
    char *fgets()    char fputs()
    int ungets()
    int fscanf()    int fprint()
    int fread()    int fwrite()
    fseek()
    ftell()
    FILE *unit, *fopen()
    unit = fopen("filename", "r")
        "r"  "w"  "a"  "r+"  "w+"  "a+"  ; (read-write)
        "rb"  "wb"  "ab"  ; (binary)
    stdin :0: standard input file
    stdout :1: standard output file
    stderr :2: standard error file
    fprintf(stdout, , , , ) = printf( , , , )
    fscanf(stdin, , , , ) = scanf( , , , )

in math.h
    double sin(double x)
    cos
    tan
    asin
```

acos
atan
atan2(double x, double y) : atan(x/y)
double sinh(double x)
cosh
tanh
exp
log
log10
sqrt
power(double x, double y) : x^y
double ceil(double x)
double floor(double x)
int abs(int x)
int rand()

Compile and Link

cc -o filexec -l library filename.c
g77 -o filexec filename.c

Appendix E

LaTeX

E.1 Basic Structure of LaTeX File

```
\documentclass[aps,preprint]{revtex4}
    % [11pt, 12pt, twoside, openbib, twocolumn, titlepage, leqno, fleqn ...]
    % {article, letter, report, slides, book ...}

\usepackage{graphicx}
\input{file}  % ; read specified file
\include{file}  % ; read specified file unless excluded by \includeonly
\includeonly{files}  % ; exclude any file not listed in files

\newdimen\epsxsize
\newcommand\epsbox[1]{\includegraphics[width=\epsxsize]{#1}}
\def\bra{\langle}
\def\ket{\rangle}

\setlength{\leftmargin}{0.5in}  % evensidemargin  oddsidemargin
\setlength{\topmargin}{-1.0cm}
\setlength{\textheight}{9.0in}
\setlength{\textwidth}{6.0in}
\setlength{\baselineskip}{4ex}
```

```
\parindent 30pt
\pagestyle{empty}  %  plain, empty, headings, myheadings
\pagenumbering{arabic}  %  arabic, roman, Roman, alph, Alph


\begin{document}


    Contents of document

\title{.....}
\author{....}
\address{....}
\maketitle

\begin{titlepage} ...... \end{titlepage}   %  ; do-it-yourself titlepage

\rightline{.....}  %  centerline
\begin{center} ..... \end{center}  %  flushleft, flushright

\begin{abstract} ........ \end{abstract}
\begin{eqnarray} ...... \end{eqnarray}
\begin{figure} ....... \end{figure}
\begin{table} ...... \end{table}
\begin{thebibliography}{99} \bibitem{ref1} ...... \end{thebibliography}

\end{document}
```

The Latex file should be compiled to convert into the final form of document. The output file is usually dvi (device independent file) and can be converted to pdf (portable document file). To compile in Unix or Linux system

latex filename.tex

For various compile options 'help latex' can be used in Unix system.

E.2 LaTeX Commands

LaTeX commands start with a back slash \. In each line of Latex file, everything coming after % are comments and the next input line follows with no blank space. The argument of a command is given in curly brackets {...}.

Document and Page Style

\documentstyle[options]{style}   % for LaTeX
\documentclass[options]{style}   % for LaTeX2E
  style :   article, report, book, slides (in SLiTeX only),
    letter (for letters), revtex4, svjour
  options : 10pt, 11pt, 12pt, twoside, twocolumn, leqno, fleqn,
    preprint, aps, titlepage, openlib, makeidx, a4paper
\pagestyle{style} : style of head and foot
    plain, empty, headings, myheadings
\pagenumbering{style} : style of page numbers
    arabic, roman, Roman, alph, Alph

Splitting the Input to Files

\input{file} : read in specified file
\include{file} : read specified file unless excluded by \includeonly
\includeonly{files} : exclude any file not listed in files
\usepackage{package} : use package   % for LaTeX2E
    hfont, graphicx, makeidx, ...

Sentences and Paragraphs

quotes : ‘......’   “......”
dashes : intra-word(-) -   number range(–) --   punctuation(—) ---
spacing : small \,   inter-word \   unbreakable ~   thin back space \!

sentence-ending period \@.
special characters : \$ \\$ & \& % \% # \#
{ \{ } \} _ _ ^ \^ \ \$\backslash\$
emphasis : {\em .....}
unbreakable text : \mbox{......}
footnotes : \footnote{.....} date : \today
blank line : start new paragraph
line break : \\
line fill : \dotfill \hrulefill

Font Style

{\bf bold face} ; **bold face**
roman \rm *italic* \it CAPS \sc *emphsis* \em *slant* \sl
`teletype` \tt **bold** \bf SSrf \sf bold math symbols \boldmath
$\mathcal{INMATHMODE}$: Calligraphic capital \cal $\mathit{\Gamma\Delta}$... \mit

Letter Size

{\small ....}
\tiny tiny \scriptsize scriptsize \footnotesize footnotesize \small small
\normalsize normalsize \large large \Large Large
\LARGE LARGE \huge huge \Huge Huge

Accents and Symbols

\`{o} ò \'{o} ó \"{o} ö \^{o} ô \~{o} õ
\={o} ō \.{o} ȯ \u{o} ŏ \v{o} ǒ \H{o} ő
\t{oo} o͡o \c{o} o̧ \d{o} ọ \b{o} o̲
\dag † dagger \ddag ‡ double dagger \S § section mark
\P ¶ paragraph mark \copyright © \pounds

Alignment

\rightline{right justify}   % \centerline
\begin{center} .... center lines ..... \end{center}
\begin{flushleft} ... left justified lines ... \end{flushleft}   % flushright

Sectioning and Table of Contents

\part   \chapter   \section   \subsection   \subsubsection
\paragraph   \subparagraph
\appendix start appendix   \tableofcontents make table of contents

Mathematical Formulas

$......$ or \(......\) : in-text formula
\[......\] : displayed formula
\begin{equation} .... \end{equation} : numbered equation
\begin{eqnarray} .... \end{eqnarray} : 3-coulum equations array
    separate columns by &
  \label{eqname} ; equation name to be referred in text by eqname
  \nonumber ; omits equation number for this line
  eqnarray* ; omits all
_{....} : subscript
^{....} : superscript
' : prime ($'$)
\frac{n}{d} : fraction $\frac{n}{d}$
\sqrt[n]{arg} : n-th root of arg $\sqrt[n]{arg}$
  \sqrt{arg} square root of arg $\sqrt{arg}$

\cdot $\cdot$ center dot   \cdots $\cdots$ \ldots $\ldots$ \vdots $\vdots$ \ddots $\ddots$
Greek letters : \alpha α \beta β \gamma γ \Gamma Γ
    \delta δ \Delta Δ .... \omega ω \Omega Ω
\nabla ∇ \sum $\sum$ \sum_{i=1}^f $\sum_{i=1}^f$ \prod $\prod$ \prod_i^f $\prod_i^f$
\vec{v} $\vec{v}$ \times $\times$ \otimes $\otimes$ \oplus $\oplus$ \cap $\cap$ \cup $\cup$
\equiv $\equiv$ \approx $\approx$ \sim $\sim$ \ne $\ne$ \| $\|$

\le $\leq$ \ge $\geq$ \ll $\ll$ \gg $\gg$

delimiters : \left ... \right \left{a+b\right} $\{a+b\}$

\left(\right) \left[\right] \left< \right> \left| \right|

\left. \right. ; To be used to complete the parenthesis pair.

\overline{expr} $\overline{expr}$

space : thin \, medium \: thick \; negative thin \!

Referencing

\label{labelname} : define a name for equation, figure, table, section, or chapter to be referred by \ref{labelname} in text

\ref{labelname} : call the number assigned to labelname in text

\cite[note]{keys} : cite references keys defined by \bibitem{key} [with added note]

\begin{thebibliography}{99} : begin reference list ; length of reference number to be same as 99, i.e. 99 is widest entry label

\bibitem[lbl]{key} : bibliography entry for citation key [with lbl as label]

\end{thebibliography}

\bibliography{....} : make bibliography and use BIBTEX

Making Index

Use documentstyle option makeidx or use \usepackage{makeidx}

\makeindex at preamble, i.e., before \begin{document}

\index{entry!subentry!subsubentry} \index{newentry|see{cross ref}}

\index{alpha@α}} ; entry is α but ordering with alpha

\index{entry|(} & \index{entry|)} ; start & end pages for an index entry

After running Latex, run makeindex texfile.idx

\printindex or \input{texfile.ind} at the position of index

Displayed Paragraphs

\begin{quote} ..... \end{quote} : short displayed quotation
\begin{quotation} ..... \end{quotation} : long displayed quotation
\begin{center} ..... \end{center} : centered lines separated by \\
\begin{verse} ..... \end{verse}
: \\ between lines, blank line between stanzas
\begin{verbatim} ..... \end{verbatim} \verb|....| or `\verb/.../`
: exactly same as formatted by key board in typewriter font

Lists

\begin{itemize} .... \end{itemize} : ticked items
\begin{enumerate} .... \end{enumerate} : numbered items
\begin{description} .... \end{description} : labeled items
\item ..... or \item[label] .....

Line Breaking

\linebreak[n] : force a line break, $0 \leq n \leq 4$
\nolinebreak[n] : forbid a line break, $0 \leq n \leq 4$
\\[len] : start new line and leave len vertical space
\- : permit hyphenation
\sloppy : allow loose lines
\begin{sloppypar} ..... \end{sloppypar} : allow loose lines in paragraphs

Page Breaking

\pagebreak[n] : force a page break, $0 \leq n \leq 4$
\nopagebreak[n] : forbid a page break, $0 \leq n \leq 4$
\samepage : forbid page breaking except between paragraphs
\newpage : start a new page
\clearpage : print all figures and tables and start a new page
\narrowtext : narrow text for two column page

Length

units ; em ex cm in mm pc pt
\newlength{cmd} : define cmd to be a length
\setlength{cmd}{len} : set length cmd to len
\addtolength{cmd}{len} : add len to length cmd
\settowidth{cmd}{txt} : set cmd to width of txt
only one setting works in one page or in one box
normal font size; 2.31ex

Space

\hspace{len} : make len horizontal space;
    \hspace*{len} works even at the beginning of line
\hfill : make infinitely stretchable horizontal space
\vspace{len} : leave len vertical space;
    \vspace*{len} works even at the beginning of page

Boxes

\mbox{....}
\makebox[wd][pos]{.....} : make box of width wd putting text at pos
    pos ; left(l), right(r), or center (default)
\fbox{text}
\framebox[wd][pos]{text} : same as \mbox or \makebox but draws frame
    around box
\newsavebox{cmd} : defines cmd be a bin for saving boxes
\sbox{cmd}{text}
\savebox{cmd}[wd][pos]{text} : same as \mbox or \makebox but saves
    box in bin cmd
\usebox{cmd} : print box saved in bin cmd
\begin{minipage}[pos]{wd}....\end{minipage} : make parbox of width wd,
    aligned by pos at top(t), bottom(b), or center (default) line
\parbox[pos]{wd}{....} : same as minipage for small text,

no displayed environments

Pictures

\unitlength
\begin{picture}$(x, y)(x', y')$ .... \end{picture} : picture of sizes $x \times y$
in unit of \unitlength with lower left corner at (x', y')
\put$(x, y)${.....} : put object given in curly brackets at point (x, y)
\multiput$(x, y)$(Deltax,Dely){n}{......} : make n copies of object with first
one at (x, y) and others offset by step of (Deltax,Dely)
\makebox$(x, y)$[pos]{....} : make $x \times y$ box at pos;
top(t), bottom (b), left (l), right (r) and centered (default)
\framebox and \savebox have analogous form
\dashbox{d}(x, y)[pos]{.....} : like \makebox but puts dashed lines of
length d around box
\line$(h, v)${l} : line with slope of diagonal $h \times v$ and horizontal extent l
(length l if $h = 0$); integer $0 \leq h, v \leq 6$
\vector$(h, v)${l} : same as \line but with arrowhead ; $0 \leq h, v \leq 4$
\circle{d} : draw circle of diameter d ; \circle*{d} for solid disk
\oval$(x, y)$[part]: draw partial oval at (x, y) : [part] ; t, b, l, r, bl ...
\shortstack[pos]{.....} : like \begin{tabular}[pos] ....
\frame{.....} : draw frame around object
line thickness : \thinlines \thicklines
\setlength{\unitlength}{0.01in} ; default length; 1 pt (point) = 1/72 inch
use this before entering picture mode

Figures and Tables

\begin{figure}[loc] .... \end{figure} : make floating figure
loc : here (h), top (t), bottom (b) of a page or full page (p)
\begin{table}[loc] ..... \end{table} : make floating table
\caption{.....} : make figure or table caption
\protect{ ... } to use some command properly in caption.

Tabbing Environment

\begin{tabbing}
\hspace{.3in}\=\hspace{0.3in}\= \hspace{0.2in}\=\kill
....
\end{tabbing}
columns determined by
\= : set tab stop
\> : go to next tab stop
\kill : throwaway line
Rows separated by \\
\' left justify when used in tabbing environment \` right justify

Array and Tabular Environments

\begin{array}[pos]{cols} .... \end{array} : use for formula
\begin{tabular}[pos]{cols} .... \end{tabular} : use for text
items separated by & and rows by \\
pos ; aligns with top (t), bottom (b), or center (default)
cols ; entries format columns :
l ; left-justified column
r ; right-justified column
c ; centered column
| ; vertical rule
@{.....} ; text or space between columns
*{n}{...} ; equivalent to n copies of ...
\multicolumn{n}{col}{.....} : span next n columns with col format
\hline : draw horizontal line between rows
\cline{i-j} : horizontal line across columns i–j

Definitions

\newcommand{cmd}[n]{.......} :

define new command cmd [with n arguments] to be ....

\newenvironment{nam}[n]{beg}{end} :
define new environment nam [with n arguments]

\newtheorem{nam}{cap} :
define a theorem-like environment nam captioned by cap

\def\defname{definition} :
define defname to be definition

Numbering

\setcounter{ctr}{n} : set counter ctr to be n
\addtocounter{ctr}{n} : add n to counter ctr
counters for page, section, etc

Mathematical Symbols

\cos	\sin	\tan	\csc	\sec	\cot
\arccos	\arcsin	\arctan	...		
\cosh	\sinh	\tanh	\coth	...	
\exp	\log	\ln	\lg		
\arg	\deg	\det	\dim	\gcd	\hom
\lim	\liminf	\limsup	\sup	\inf	\Pr
\min	\max	\ker			

\matrix{a & b & c \cr d & e & f \cr g & h & i } $\Longrightarrow$ $\matrix{a & b & c \cr d & e & f \cr g & h & i}$

\pmatrix{a & b & c \cr d & e & f \cr g & h & i } $\Longrightarrow$ $\begin{pmatrix} a & b & c \\ d & e & f \\ g & h & i \end{pmatrix}$

\bordermatrix{a & b & c \cr d & e & f \cr g & h & i } $\Longrightarrow$ $\bordermatrix{a & b & c \cr d & e & f \cr g & h & i}$

α	\alpha	β	\beta	γ	\gamma	δ	\delta
ϵ	\epsilon	ε	\varepsilon	ζ	\zeta	η	\eta
θ	\theta	ϑ	\vartheta	ι	\iota	κ	\kappa
λ	\lamda	μ	\mu	ν	\nu	ξ	\xi
o	o	π	\pi	ϖ	\varpi	ρ	\rho
ϱ	\varrho	σ	\sigma	ς	\varsigma	τ	\tau
υ	\upsilon	ϕ	\phi	φ	\varphi	χ	\chi
ψ	\psi	ω	\omega				

Γ	\Gamma	Δ	\Delta	Θ	\Theta	Λ	\Lambda
Ξ	\Xi	Π	\Pi	Σ	\Sigma	Υ	\Upsilon
Φ	\Phi	Ψ	\Psi	Ω	\Omega		

$\mathit{\Gamma}$	\mit\Gamma	$\mathit{\Delta}$	\mit\Delta	$\mathit{\Theta}$	\mit\Theta	$\cdots$	

Calligraphic capitals : {\cal CAL} $\mathcal{CAL}$

$\aleph$	\aleph	$\hbar$	\hbar	$\imath$	\imath	$\jmath$	\jmath
ℓ	\ell	$\wp$	\wp	$\Re$	\Re	$\Im$	\Im
∂	\partial	∞	\infty	$\prime$	\prime	$\emptyset$	\emptyset
∇	\nabla	$\surd$	\surd	$\top$	\top	$\bot$	\bot
$\|$	|	$\angle$	\angle	$\triangle$	\triangle	$\backslash$	\backslash
$\forall$	\forall	$\exists$	\exists	$\neg$	\neg or \lnot	$\hat\imath$	\hat\imath
$\natural$	\natural	$\sharp$	\sharp	$\flat$	\flat	$\hat\jmath$	\hat\jmath
$\clubsuit$	\clubsuit	$\heartsuit$	\heartsuit	$\diamondsuit$	\diamondsuit	$\spadesuit$	\spadesuit

Large operators, comes in two sizes :

$\sum$	\sum	$\prod$	\prod	$\coprod$	\coprod	$\int$	\int
$\oint$	\oint	$\bigcap$	\bigcap	$\bigcup$	\bigcub	$\bigsqcup$	\bigsqcup
$\bigvee$	\bigvee	$\bigwedge$	\bigwedge	$\bigodot$	\bigodot	$\bigotimes$	\bigotimes
$\bigoplus$	\bigoplus	$\biguplus$	\biguplus				

Smaller symbols :

Σ	`\Sigma`	Π	`\Pi`	$\amalg$	`\amalg`	$\smallint$	`\smallint`

Binary operators:

$\pm$	`\pm`	$\mp$	`\mp`	$\setminus$	`\setminus`
$\cdot$	`\cdot`	$\times$	`\times`	$\ast$	`\ast`
$\star$	`\star`	$\diamond$	`\diamond`	$\circ$	`\circ`
$\bullet$	`\bullet`	$\div$	`\div`	$\cap$	`\cap`
$\cup$	`\cup`	$\uplus$	`\uplus`	$\sqcap$	`\sqcap`
$\sqcup$	`\sqcup`	$\triangleleft$	`\triangleleft`	$\triangleright$	`\triangleright`
$\wr$	`\wr`	$\bigcirc$	`\bigcirc`	$\bigtriangleup$	`\bigtriangleup`
$\bigtriangledown$	`\bigtriangledown`	$\vee$	`\vee` or `\lor`	$\wedge$	`\wedge` or `\land`
$\oplus$	`\oplus`	$\ominus$	`\ominus`	$\otimes$	`\otimes`
$\oslash$	`\oslash`	$\odot$	`\odot`	$\amalg$	`\amalg`
$\dagger$	`\dagger`	$\ddagger$	`\ddagger`	$\neg$	`\neg` or `\lnot`

Relations :

$\equiv$	`\equiv`	$\sim$	`\sim`	$\simeq$	`\simeq`
$\approx$	`\approx`	$\asymp$	`\asymp`	$\cong$	`\cong`
$\doteq$	`\doteq`	$\propto$	`\propto`	$\bowtie$	`\bowtie`
$\models$	`\models`	$\ll$	`\ll`	$\gg$	`\gg`
$\leq$	`\leq` or `\le`	$\geq$	`\geq` or `\ge`	$\prec$	`\prec`
$\succ$	`\succ`	$\preceq$	`\preceq`	$\succeq$	`\succeq`
$\subset$	`\subset`	$\supset$	`\supset`	$\subseteq$	`\subseteq`
$\supseteq$	`\supseteq`	$\sqsubseteq$	`\sqsubseteq`	$\sqsupseteq$	`\sqsupseteq`
$\in$	`\in`	$\vdash$	`\vdash`	$\smile$	`\smile`
$\ni$	`\ni` or `\owns`	$\dashv$	`\dashv`	$\frown$	`\frown`
$\mid$	`\mid` or `|` or `\vert`	$\parallel$	`\parallel` or `\\|`	$\perp$	`\perp`

Negated relations :

$\neq$	`\not=` or `\ne` or `\neq`	$\not\equiv$	`\not\equiv`	$\not\sim$	`\not\sim`
$\not\simeq$	`\not\simeq`	$\not\approx$	`\not\approx`	$\not\cong$	`\not\cong`

$\not\asymp$	\not\asymp	$\not<$	\not<	$\not>$	\not>
$\not\leq$	\not\leq	$\not\geq$	\not\geq	$\not\prec$	\not\prec
$\not\succ$	\not\succ	$\not\preceq$	\not\preceq	$\not\succeq$	\not\succeq
$\not\subset$	\not\subset	$\not\supset$	\not\supset	$\not\subseteq$	\not\subseteq
$\not\supseteq$	\not\supseteq	$\not\sqsubseteq$	\not\sqsubseteq	$\not\supseteq$	\not\supseteq

Arrows :

$\leftarrow$	\leftarrow or \gets	$\longleftarrow$	\longleftarrow	$\uparrow$	\uparrow
$\Leftarrow$	\Leftarrow	$\Longleftarrow$	\Longleftarrow	$\Uparrow$	\Uparrow
$\rightarrow$	\rightarrow or \to	$\longrightarrow$	\longrightarrow	$\downarrow$	\downarrow
$\Rightarrow$	\Rightarrow	$\Longrightarrow$	\Longrightarrow	$\Downarrow$	\Downarrow
$\leftrightarrow$	\leftrightarrow	$\longleftrightarrow$	\ongleftrightarrow	$\updownarrow$	\updownarrow
$\Leftrightarrow$	\Leftrightarrow	$\Longleftrightarrow$	\Longleftrightarrow	$\Updownarrow$	\Updownarrow
$\mapsto$	\mapsto	$\longmapsto$	\longmapsto	$\nearrow$	\nearrow
$\hookleftarrow$	\hookleftarrow	$\hookrightarrow$	\hookrightarrow	$\searrow$	\searrow
$\leftharpoonup$	\leftharpoonup	$\rightharpoonup$	\rightharpoonup	$\swarrow$	\swarrow
$\leftharpoondown$	\leftharpoondown	$\rightharpoondown$	\rightharpoondown	$\nwarrow$	\nwarrow
$\rightleftharpoons$	\rightleftharpoons	$\buildrel \rm def \over =$	\buildrel \rm def \over =		

Additives on top of letter :

$\vec V$	\vec V	$\hat h$	\hat h	$\bar b$	\bar b	$\tilde t$	\tilde t

Openings and closings :

$[$	\lbrack or \[	$\{$	\lbrace or \{	$\langle$	\langle
$\lfloor$	\lfloor	$\lceil$	\lceil		\left.
$]$	\rbrack or \]	$\}$	\rbrace or \}	$\rangle$	\rangle
$\rfloor$	\rfloor	$\rceil$	\rceil		\right.
$\lbrack\!\lbrack$	\lbrack\!\lbrack	$\langle\!\langle$	\langle\!\langle	$(\!($	(\!(

Symbols with abnormal spacing :

\ldotp : . with the spacing of commas and semicolons.

\cdotp : $\cdotp$ with the spacing of commas and semicolons.
\iff : $\iff$ with an extra thick space at each side.

Non-math symbols :

§ \S	¶ \P	† \dag	‡ \ddag

E.3 Sample LaTeX

LaTeX2E file : sample.tex

```
\documentclass[aps,preprint]{revtex4}
%\documentclass[aps]{revtex4}
%\documentclass[aps,twocolumn]{revtex4}


\usepackage{graphicx}
\newdimen\epsfxsize
\newcommand\epsfbox[1]{\includegraphics[width=\epsfxsize]{#1}}
\def\figsiz{3.0in}
\def\figsiz{5.0in}
\def\bra{\langle}
\def\ket{\rangle}

\parindent 30pt
%\setlength{\leftmargin}{-0.7in}
\setlength{\evensidemargin}{0.2in}
\setlength{\oddsidemargin}{0.2in}
\setlength{\textwidth}{6.0in}
\setlength{\textheight}{8.0in}
\setlength{\topmargin}{0.2in}
\setlength{\baselineskip}{4ex}

\pagestyle{plain} % plain, empty, headings, myheadings
\pagenumbering{arabic}  % arabic, roman, alph, Roman, Alph


\begin{document}


\rightline{\today}
```

```
\title{Neutron Skin Size Dependence of the Nuclear Symmetry
Energy}

\author{ S.J. Lee\footnote{Email: leexxx@khu.ac.kr}}

\affiliation
{Department of Physics and Institute of Natural Sciences,
         Kyung Hee University, Suwon, KyungGiDo, Korea}

\author{A. Z. Mekjian}

\affiliation
{Department of Physics and Astronomy, Rutgers University,
Piscataway, NJ 08854, USA}


\begin{abstract}

The nuclear binding energy with emphasis on the symmetry
energy is studied using a finite temperature density
functional theory. A Skyrme interaction is used in this work.
Volume, surface, and symmetry energy contributions to the
binding energy are investigated.  \\
 .........  \\
The neutron-skin-size-dependent parts of the symmetry energy
coefficients have the same sign as the neutron-skin-independent
parts, which indicates that a larger neutron skin causes a
lager symmetry energy.

\end{abstract}

\pacs{PACS no.: 21.10.Dr, 21.10.Gv, 21.60.Jz, 21.65.-f}

\keywords{Binding energy, Symmetry energy, Surface energy,
   Temperature dependence, Neutron skin size dependence}
```

```
\maketitle


\section{Introduction}

The mass formulae \cite{ref1,ref7,dan9,dan11} characterize the
binding energy of nuclei in terms of the proton number $Z$
and the neutron number $N$ or the nucleon number $A=Z+N$.
Volume, surface, Coulomb and pairing terms appear.
Of importance and one of the least determined parts of
the binding energy expression is the symmetry
energy term. The symmetry energy has both a volume
symmetry part and a surface symmetry part,
similar to the division of the volume and the surface terms.
The division into volume and surface energies occurs because
observed nuclei have finite nucleon numbers with a maximum
value of $A \sim 250$.
The symmetry energy appears in the total binding energy
with factors involving
both $((N-Z)/A)^2 A$ and $((N-Z)/A)^2 A^{2/3}$ for
the volume and the surface symmetry terms, respectively. \\
  ...........  \\
Extensive discussion of the symmetry energy can be found in
the work of Danielewicz and Lee \cite{daniel}. The role of
the symmetry energy in the nuclear surface has also been
studied in Ref.\cite{daniel}.
An extensive review can be found in Ref.\cite{praka}.

In this paper, we study the effect of the neutron skin on
the volume and the surface contributions to the symmetry
energy. Our approach is based on a finite-temperature density
functional theory, and we use a Skyrme type of interaction
which we develop in the next
section. The same Skyrme approach was also used to study phase
transitions in Ref.\cite{prc79,prc77,pl580,prc68}.
```

```
The symmetry energy and the neutron-skin effects on the
symmetry energy and the other energy coefficients for three
cases of Skyrme interactions are
studied in Sect. \ref{result}, and
the results are summarized in Sect. \ref{concl}.


\section{Binding energy in a density functional approach}

A density functional theory based on a Skyrme interaction,
which is summarized in Appendix \ref{appena},
will be used in our investigation.
The density distribution is taken to be of the Saxon-Wood form:
\begin{eqnarray}
 \rho_q(\vec r) = \rho_q(R_q)
    = \frac{\rho_{qc}}{1 + e^{(r - R_q)/a_q}}  .
                              \label{fermden}
\end{eqnarray}
The $q = p, n$ for protons, neutrons.
We will allow the central density $\rho_{qc}$ and the $R_q$
for protons and neutrons to be different in general.
The diffusenesses $a_q$ are taken to be the same
for simplicity because our focus is on the neutron-skin-size
dependence rather than the effects of different diffusenesses.
%
For the density of Eq. (\ref{fermden}),
 $<r^2>_q = \frac{3}{5} R_q^2 \left[1 + \frac{7}{3}
               \left(\frac{\pi a_q}{R_q}\right)^2\right]$.
The contribution of the diffuseness $a_q$ to the
root-mean-square radius is less than 1/4 the rms radius
even for a small nucleus of $A = 20$.
This means that taking the same diffuseness should not affect
our result much, at least qualitatively.
Two limiting cases can also be considered:
(1) $R_p = R_n$ so that the difference in $N \ne Z$ nuclei is
in the central density or $\rho_{pc} \ne \rho_{nc}$
```

```
and (2) $R_p \ne R_n$ with $\rho_{pc} = \rho_{nc}$.
In case 2, the neutron distribution reflects a neutron skin
for $N > Z$.


\begin{table}
%\vspace*{-0.85in}
\caption{Neutron skin dependence of the energy coefficient
minimizing the Helmholtz free energy. }  \label{tabl1}
\hspace*{-0.3in}
\begin{tabular}{l|rrr|rrr|rrrr}
\hline
                 &   \multicolumn{3}{|c}{SLy4}
                 &   \multicolumn{3}{|c}{SkM$^*$}
                 &   \multicolumn{3}{|c}{SkM($m^*=m$)}      \\
\hline
 $T$ (MeV)      &  0 \ \ \ &  1 \ \ \ &  2 \ \ \
                &  0 \ \ \ &  1 \ \ \ &  2 \ \ \
                &  0 \ \ \ &  1 \ \ \ &  2 \ \ \ \\
\hline
 $E_V(T)$       & --15.308 & --15.296 & --15.263
                & --15.127 & --15.108 & --15.051
                & --15.310 & --15.270 & --15.152  \\
 \ \ $E_V$      & --15.308 & --15.308 & --15.308
                & --15.127 & --15.127 & --15.127
                & --15.310 & --15.310 & --15.310  \\
 \ \ $EK_{V,T}$ &  0.01151 &  0.01145 &  0.01121
                &  0.01925 &  0.01921 &  0.01908
                &  0.03948 &  0.03948 &  0.03950  \\
 \ \ $EK_V(T)$  &  28.653  &  28.594  &  28.423
                &  25.483  &  25.444  &  25.319
                &  19.957  &  19.978  &  20.037   \\
 $E_{V,t}(T)$   &  5.5202  &  5.5100  &  5.4792
                &  5.5837  &  5.5730  &  5.5411
                &  6.9809  &  6.9701  &  6.9379   \\
 \ \ $E_{V,t}$  &  5.5202  &  5.5172  &  5.5081
```

```
                & 5.5837 & 5.5806 & 5.5717
                & 6.9809 & 6.9780 & 6.9697  \\
 \ \ $EK_{V,T,t}$&--0.00722 &--0.00722 &--0.00723
                &--0.00761 &--0.00762 &--0.00763
                &--0.00793 &--0.00793 &--0.00793  \\
 \ \ $EK_{V,t}(T)$&--3.8780 & --3.8654 & --3.8269
                & --0.4893 & --0.4995 & --0.5302
                & --0.3867 & --0.3963 & --0.4253  \\
\hline
\end{tabular}
\end{table}


Using this density functional approach, the binding energy of
nuclei as a function of mass number $A$, proton number $Z$
and temperature $T$ can be evaluated.
The Weizacker semiemperical mass formulae \cite{ref1},
its extension by Myers and Swiatecki
 \cite{dan10,dan14,dan15,dan16},
and including finite temperature effects \cite{prc82} is
\begin{eqnarray}
 E(A,Z,T)
  &=& E_V(T) A + E_S(T) A^{2/3} + S_V(T) I^2 A +
        S_S(T) I^2 A^{2/3}
           \nonumber \\    & &
     + E_C \frac{Z^2}{A^{1/3}} + E_{dif} \frac{Z^2}{A}
     + E_{ex} \frac{Z^{4/3}}{A^{1/3}} + c \Delta A^{-1/2} ,
                \label{ldexpan}
\end{eqnarray}
where $I = (N-Z)/A = (A - 2Z)/A$.
The $B = -E_V$ is the usual bulk energy per nucleon.
The $E_{dif}$ and the $E_{ex}$ are the coefficients for
the diffuseness correction and the exchange correction to
the Coulomb energy, respectively.
For the pairing correction with constant $\Delta$, $c = +1$
for odd-odd nuclei, 0 for odd-even nuclei,
```

```
and $-1$ for even-even nuclei.
%
The above formula at $T =0$ is the well-known Weizacker
semiempirical mass formula \cite{ref1,ref7,dan9,dan11}
studied extensively by Myers and
Swiatecki \cite{dan10,dan14,dan15,dan16}.
Early studies excluded the surface
symmetry term $S_S$, and only the surface term $E_S$ was
included. The values of the coefficients,
as found in textbooks such as Ref.\cite{ref7} and \cite{dan11}
are $E_V(0) = -B(0) \approx -16$, $E_S(0) \approx 17$,
and $S_V(0) \approx 24$ in MeV.
The ratio $E_S/B$ of surface to bulk energy at $T=0$ is
very close to unity.


\section{Neutron skin size dependence}  \label{result}

Here, we examine the neutron-skin-size dependence of nuclear
energy by using various Skyrme interactions to minimize
Helmholtz free energy
for various nuclei along the beta-stability line \cite{prc82}.
We used three sets of Skyrme parameters from our previous
paper \cite{prc82} with different values of the
effective mass in symmetric nuclear matter:
SLy4 with $m^*/m = 0.69$, SkM$^*$ with $m^*/m = 0.79$,
and SkM($m^*=m$) with $m^*/m = 1$.
The results for these three cases are given
in Table \ref{tabl1}. The three cases cover a wide range of
interaction types in terms
of effective mass within the many various Skyrme interactions.
In a previous paper \cite{prc82}, we found that the energy
expansion coefficients were insensitive to the temperature and
the interaction used except for a dependence on the effective
mass of the interaction.
This feature was seen by taking a Skyrme with $m^*/m = 1$ and
```

```
comparing it to the other cases SkM$^*$ and SLy4, together
with some more cases with different effective masses
in Ref.\cite{prc82}.


\begin{figure}

\includegraphics[width=3.0in]{Fig1}

\caption{The total symmetry energy
$E_{sym}(T) = S_V(T) I^2 A + S_S(T) I^2 A^{2/3}$
in MeV versus mass number $A$ along the line of stability.
The upper curves are the interaction SLy4 (the solid curve
for $T=0$ and the dashed curve for $T=3$ MeV) and the
lower curves are SKM($m^*=m$) (the dash-dotted curve for
$T=0$ and the dash-dot-dot-dotted curve for $T=3$ MeV).
The dotted curve is a pure volume term symmetry energy
with $S_V = 24$ MeV and $S_S =0$ MeV.
The $E_{sym,\beta}$ is in MeV.
  }    \label{fig1}
\end{figure}


\begin{figure}
%\includegraphics[width=5.0in]{Fig2}
\centerline{
   \epsfxsize=2.0in  \epsfbox{Fig2}
     }

\caption{Comparison of a symmetry energy with both volume
and surface terms and a symmetry energy with just a volume
term for SLy4 interaction. The symmetry energy is calculated
along the line of $\beta$ stability.
The upper and lower figures are the difference
$\Delta E_{sym,\beta}$ and $\Delta E_{sym,\beta}/A$
in MeV between the two symmetry energies
```

```
with both volume and surface symmetry energy terms for
SLy4 interaction and with volume symmetry energy term only
(dotted curve in Fig.\ref{fig1}).
The solid curve is at $T=0$, the dashed curve at $T=1$,
the dash-dotted curve at $T=2$, and the dash-dot-dot-dotted
curve at $T=3$ MeV.
At $A = 100$ and $T = 0$, the SLy4 interaction gives a total
symmetry energy of 43.09 MeV, while the pure volume
calculation has 46.44 MeV.
   }
          \label{fig2}
\end{figure}


\section{Conclusion and summary}  \label{concl}

Understanding the properties of the symmetry energy is
important in many areas of nuclear physics, as mentioned
in the introduction.
In this paper, we studied the properties of the symmetry
energy, both the volume and the surface parts, along with
those of the other terms that appear in the Weizsacker
mass formulae.   \\
   ..............

This work was supported in part by Grant No. KHU-xxxxxxx
of the Kyung Hee University Research Fund in 2008
and by the US Department of Energy under DOE Grant
No. DE-xxxxxx-xxxxx.


\appendix


\section{Skyrme Interaction} \label{appena}
```

```
The Hamiltonian for a Skyrme interaction is
\begin{eqnarray}
 H(\vec r) &=& H_B(\vec r) + H_S(\vec r) + H_C(\vec r)   ,
       \label{hamilt}
\end{eqnarray}
where the details of the bulk part $H_B(\vec r)$,
the surface part $H_S(\vec r)$ with gradient terms, and
the Coulomb term $H_C(\vec r)$ are given in our previous
paper \cite{prc82}.
The explicit temperature dependence comes in through the
kinetic energy factor
$\tau_q = \sum_{j \epsilon q} |i \vec\nabla \psi_j|^2
   = \int \frac{p^2}{\hbar^2} f_q(\vec r, \vec p) d^3p$,
where $q = n, p$ for neutrons or protons.
At low $T$, the degenerate Fermi gas model gives
 ..............   \\
 .................


\section{Expansion of Density}  \label{appenrho}

The central density $\rho_{qc}$ of the density distribution
for a given value of $R_q$ should be determined to give a
fixed number of nucleons $N_q$:
\begin{eqnarray}
 N_q(R_q) &=& \rho_{qc}(R_q) \frac{4\pi}{3} R_q^3 \left[1
       + \pi^2 \left(\frac{a}{R_q}\right)^2\right]
                \label{nqnorm}
\end{eqnarray}
for the density of Eq.(\ref{fermden}).
This normalization condition gives, up to first order
in $dR_q = (R_q - R)$,
\begin{eqnarray}
 \rho_{qc}(R_q) &\approx& \rho_{qc}(R) \left[1
      - \left(\frac{3 + \pi^2 \left(\frac{a}{R}\right)^2}
             {1 + \pi^2 \left(\frac{a}{R}\right)^2}\right)
```

```
        \left(\frac{R_q - R}{R}\right) \right] .
 \label{rhoqc}
\end{eqnarray}
Thus, the first-order correction coefficient to the $m$-th
power $\rho_{qc}^m$ of $\rho_{qc}$ due to fixed $N_q$ is
the zeroth-order term times
$-\frac{m}{R} \left[\frac{3 + \pi^2 \left(\frac{a}{R}
  \right)^2} {1 + \pi^2 \left(\frac{a}{R}\right)^2}\right]$.
This result is independent of which type of particle,
neutron or proton.
 ..........   \\
  ................


\begin{thebibliography}{99}

\bibitem{ref1} C. F. Weizsacker, Z. Phys. {\bf 96}, 431 (1935)
\bibitem{ref7} A. Bohr and B. R. Mottelson, {\bf Nuclear
         Structure}, Vol I (Benjamin, New York, 1969).
\bibitem{dan9} H. A. Bethe and R. F. Bacher, Rev. Mod. Phys.
        {\bf 8}, 82 (1936).
\bibitem{dan11} M. A. Preston and R. K. Bhaduri,
      {\bf Structure of the Nucleus} (Addison Wesley, Reading,
       MA, 1975).

\bibitem{praka} A. W. Steiner, M. Prakash, J. M. Lattimer,
         and P. J. Ellis, Phys. Rep. {\bf 411}, 325 (2005).
\bibitem{daniel} P. Danielewicz and J. Lee, Int. J. Mod. Phys.
      E{\bf 18}, 829 (2009)  (Nucl. Phys. A{\bf 818},
      36 (2009)).

\bibitem{prc82} S. J. Lee and A. Z. Mekjian,
         Phys. Rev. C{\bf 82}, 064319 (2010).
\bibitem{prc79} S. J. Lee and A. Z. Mekjian,
         Phys. Rev. C{\bf 79}, 044323 (2009).
\bibitem{prc77} S. J. Lee and A. Z. Mekjian,
```

```
        Phys. Rev. C{\bf 77}, 054612 (2008).
\bibitem{pl580} S. J. Lee and A. Z. Mekjian, Phys. Lett.
        {\bf 580}, 137 (2004).
\bibitem{prc68} S. J. Lee and A. Z. Mekjian,
        Phys. Rev. C{\bf 68}, 014608 (2003).
\bibitem{dan10} W. D. Myers, W. J. Swiatecki, Nucl. Phys.
        A{\bf 81}, 1 (1966).
\bibitem{dan14} W. D. Myers, W. J. Swiatecki, Ann. Phys.
        {\bf 55}, 395 (1969).
\bibitem{dan15} W. D. Myers, W. J. Swiatecki, Ann. Phys.
        {\bf 84}, 186 (1974).
\bibitem{dan16} W. D. Myers, {\bf Droplet Model of Atomic
        Nuclei}, IFI/Plenum, New York, 1975.

\end{thebibliography}


\end{document}
```

Result : compiled in unix system ; latex sample.tex

November 25, 2013

Neutron Skin Size Dependence of the Nuclear Symmetry Energy

S.J. Lee*

Department of Physics and Institute of Natural Sciences,

Kyung Hee University, Suwon, KyungGiDo, Korea

A. Z. Mekjian

Department of Physics and Astronomy,

Rutgers University, Piscataway, NJ 08854, USA

Abstract

The nuclear binding energy with emphasis on the symmetry energy is studied using a finite temperature density functional theory. A Skyrme interaction is used in this work. Volume, surface, and symmetry energy contributions to the binding energy are investigated.

....

The neutron-skin-size-dependent parts of the symmetry energy coefficients have the same sign as the neutron-skin-independent parts, which indicates that a larger neutron skin causes a lager symmetry energy.

*Email: leexxx@khu.ac.kr

I. INTRODUCTION

The mass formulae [1–4] characterize the binding energy of nuclei in terms of the proton number Z and the neutron number N or the nucleon number $A = Z + N$. Volume, surface, Coulomb and pairing terms appear. Of importance and one of the least determined parts of the binding energy expression is the symmetry energy term. The symmetry energy has both a volume symmetry part and a surface symmetry part, similar to the division of the volume and the surface terms. The division into volume and surface energies occurs because observed nuclei have finite nucleon numbers with a maximum value of $A \sim 250$. The symmetry energy appears in the total binding energy with factors involving both $((N - Z)/A)^2 A$ and $((N - Z)/A)^2 A^{2/3}$ for the volume and the surface symmetry terms, respectively.

....

Extensive discussion of the symmetry energy can be found in the work of Danielewicz and Lee [6]. The role of the symmetry energy in the nuclear surface has also been studied in Ref.[6]. An extensive review can be found in Ref.[5].

In this paper, we study the effect of the neutron skin on the volume and the surface contributions to the symmetry energy. Our approach is based on a finite-temperature density functional theory, and we use a Skyrme type of interaction which we develop in the next section. The same Skyrme approach was also used to study phase transitions in Ref.[8–11]. The symmetry energy and the neutron-skin effects on the symmetry energy and the other energy coefficients for three cases of Skyrme interactions are studied in Sect. III, and the results are summarized in Sect. IV.

II. BINDING ENERGY IN A DENSITY FUNCTIONAL APPROACH

A density functional theory based on a Skyrme interaction, which is summarized in Appendix A, will be used in our investigation. The density distribution is taken to be of the Saxon-Wood form:

$$\rho_q(\vec{r}) = \rho_q(R_q) = \frac{\rho_{qc}}{1 + e^{(r-R_q)/a_q}}. \tag{1}$$

The $q = p, n$ for protons, neutrons. We will allow the central density ρ_{qc} and the R_q for protons and neutrons to be different in general. The diffusenesses a_q are taken to be the same for simplicity because our focus is on the neutron-skin-size dependence rather than the effects of different diffusenesses. For the density of Eq. (1), $< r^2 >_q = \frac{3}{5}R_q^2 \left[1 + \frac{7}{3}\left(\frac{\pi a_q}{R_q}\right)^2\right]$. The contribution of the diffuseness a_q to the root-mean-square radius is less than 1/4 the rms radius even for a small nucleus of $A = 20$. This means that taking the same diffuseness should not affect our result much, at least qualitatively. Two limiting cases can also be considered: (1) $R_p = R_n$ so that the difference in $N \neq Z$ nuclei is in the central density or $\rho_{pc} \neq \rho_{nc}$ and (2) $R_p \neq R_n$ with $\rho_{pc} = \rho_{nc}$. In case 2, the neutron distribution reflects a neutron skin for $N > Z$.

Using this density functional approach, the binding energy of nuclei as a function of mass number A, proton number Z and temperature T can be evaluated. The Weizacker semiemperical mass formulae [1], its extension by Myers and Swiatecki [12–15], and including finite temperature effects [7] is

$$\begin{aligned} E(A,Z,T) &= E_V(T)A + E_S(T)A^{2/3} + S_V(T)I^2A + S_S(T)I^2A^{2/3} \\ &\quad + E_C\frac{Z^2}{A^{1/3}} + E_{dif}\frac{Z^2}{A} + E_{ex}\frac{Z^{4/3}}{A^{1/3}} + c\Delta A^{-1/2}, \end{aligned} \tag{2}$$

where $I = (N - Z)/A = (A - 2Z)/A$. The $B = -E_V$ is the usual bulk energy per nucleon. The E_{dif} and the E_{ex} are the coefficients for the diffuseness correction and the exchange correction to the Coulomb energy, respectively. For the pairing correction with constant Δ, $c = +1$ for odd-odd nuclei, 0 for odd-even nuclei, and -1 for even-even nuclei. The above formula at $T = 0$ is the well-known Weizacker semiempirical mass formula [1–4] studied extensively by Myers and Swiatecki [12–15]. Early studies excluded the surface symmetry term S_S, and only the surface term E_S

TABLE I: Neutron skin dependence of the energy coefficient minimizing the Helmholtz free energy.

	SLy4			SkM*			SkM($m^* = m$)		
T (MeV)	0	1	2	0	1	2	0	1	2
$E_V(T)$	-15.308	-15.296	-15.263	-15.127	-15.108	-15.051	-15.310	-15.270	-15.152
E_V	-15.308	-15.308	-15.308	-15.127	-15.127	-15.127	-15.310	-15.310	-15.310
$EK_{V,T}$	0.01151	0.01145	0.01121	0.01925	0.01921	0.01908	0.03948	0.03948	0.03950
$EK_V(T)$	28.653	28.594	28.423	25.483	25.444	25.319	19.957	19.978	20.037
$E_{V,t}(T)$	5.5202	5.5100	5.4792	5.5837	5.5730	5.5411	6.9809	6.9701	6.9379
$E_{V,t}$	5.5202	5.5172	5.5081	5.5837	5.5806	5.5717	6.9809	6.9780	6.9697
$EK_{V,T,t}$	-0.00722	-0.00722	-0.00723	-0.00761	-0.00762	-0.00763	-0.00793	-0.00793	-0.00793
$EK_{V,t}(T)$	-3.8780	-3.8654	-3.8269	-0.4893	-0.4995	-0.5302	-0.3867	-0.3963	-0.4253

was included. The values of the coefficients, as found in textbooks such as Ref.[2] and [4] are $E_V(0) = -B(0) \approx -16$, $E_S(0) \approx 17$, and $S_V(0) \approx 24$ in MeV. The ratio E_S/B of surface to bulk energy at $T = 0$ is very close to unity.

III. NEUTRON SKIN SIZE DEPENDENCE

Here, we examine the neutron-skin-size dependence of nuclear energy by using various Skyrme interactions to minimize Helmholtz free energy for various nuclei along the beta-stability line [7]. We used three sets of Skyrme parameters from our previous paper [7] with different values of the effective mass in symmetric nuclear matter: SLy4 with $m^*/m = 0.69$, SkM* with $m^*/m = 0.79$, and SkM($m^* = m$) with $m^*/m = 1$. The results for these three cases are given in Table I. The three cases cover a wide range of interaction types in terms of effective mass within the many various Skyrme interactions. In a previous paper [7], we found that the energy expansion coefficients were insensitive to the temperature and the interaction used except for a dependence on the effective mass of the interaction. This feature was seen by taking a Skyrme with $m^*/m = 1$ and comparing it to the other cases SkM* and SLy4, together with some more cases with different effective masses in Ref.[7].

IV. CONCLUSION AND SUMMARY

Understanding the properties of the symmetry energy is important in many areas of nuclear physics, as mentioned in the introduction. In this paper, we studied the properties of the symmetry energy, both the volume and the surface parts, along with those of the other terms that appear in the Weizsacker mass formulae.

....

This work was supported in part by Grant No. KHU-xxxxxxx of the Kyung Hee University Research Fund in 2008 and by the US Department of Energy under DOE Grant No. DE-xxxxxx-xxxxx.

APPENDIX A: SKYRME INTERACTION

The Hamiltonian for a Skyrme interaction is

$$H(\vec{r}) = H_B(\vec{r}) + H_S(\vec{r}) + H_C(\vec{r}), \tag{A1}$$

where the details of the bulk part $H_B(\vec{r})$, the surface part $H_S(\vec{r})$ with gradient terms, and the Coulomb term $H_C(\vec{r})$ are given in our previous paper [7]. The explicit temperature dependence comes in through the kinetic energy factor $\tau_q = \sum_{j\epsilon q} |i\vec{\nabla}\psi_j|^2 = \int \frac{p^2}{\hbar^2} f_q(\vec{r}, \vec{p}) d^3p$, where $q = n, p$ for neutrons or protons. At low T, the degenerate Fermi gas model gives ....

....

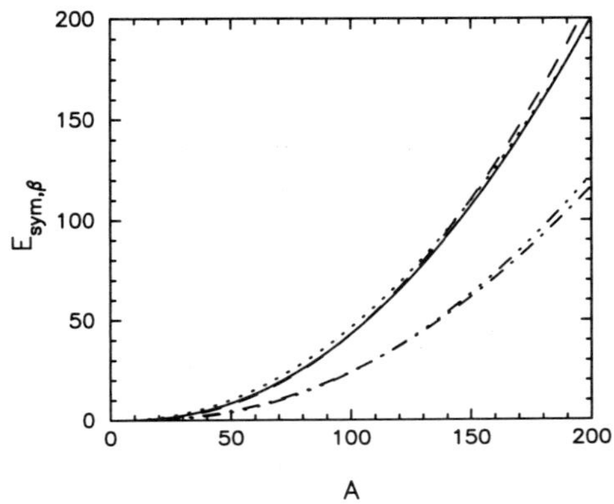

FIG. 1: The total symmetry energy $E_{sym}(T) = S_V(T)I^2A + S_S(T)I^2A^{2/3}$ in MeV versus mass number A along the line of stability. The upper curves are the interaction SLy4 (the solid curve for $T = 0$ and the dashed curve for $T = 3$ MeV) and the lower curves are SKM($m^* = m$) (the dash-dotted curve for $T = 0$ and the dash-dot-dot-dotted curve for $T = 3$ MeV). The dotted curve is a pure volume term symmetry energy with $S_V = 24$ MeV and $S_S = 0$ MeV. The $E_{sym,\beta}$ is in MeV.

APPENDIX B: EXPANSION OF DENSITY

The central density ρ_{qc} of the density distribution for a given value of R_q should be determined to give a fixed number of nucleons N_q:

$$N_q(R_q) = \rho_{qc}(R_q)\frac{4\pi}{3}R_q^3\left[1+\pi^2\left(\frac{a}{R_q}\right)^2\right] \tag{B1}$$

for the density of Eq.(1). This normalization condition gives, up to first order in $dR_q = (R_q - R)$,

$$\rho_{qc}(R_q) \approx \rho_{qc}(R)\left[1-\left(\frac{3+\pi^2\left(\frac{a}{R}\right)^2}{1+\pi^2\left(\frac{a}{R}\right)^2}\right)\left(\frac{R_q-R}{R}\right)\right]. \tag{B2}$$

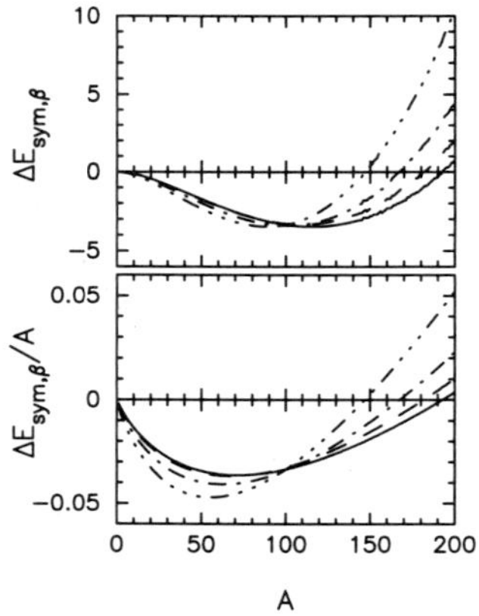

FIG. 2: Comparison of a symmetry energy with both volume and surface terms and a symmetry energy with just a volume term for SLy4 interaction. The symmetry energy is calculated along the line of β stability. The upper and lower figures are the difference $\Delta E_{sym,\beta}$ and $\Delta E_{sym,\beta}/A$ in MeV between the two symmetry energies with both volume and surface symmetry energy terms for SLy4 interaction and with volume symmetry energy term only (dotted curve in Fig.1). The solid curve is at $T = 0$, the dashed curve at $T = 1$, the dash-dotted curve at $T = 2$, and the dash-dot-dot-dotted curve at $T = 3$ MeV. At $A = 100$ and $T = 0$, the SLy4 interaction gives a total symmetry energy of 43.09 MeV, while the pure volume calculation has 46.44 MeV.

Thus, the first-order correction coefficient to the m-th power ρ_{qc}^m of ρ_{qc} due to fixed N_q is the zeroth-order term times $-\frac{m}{R}\left[\frac{3+\pi^2\left(\frac{a}{R}\right)^2}{1+\pi^2\left(\frac{a}{R}\right)^2}\right]$. This result is independent of which type of particle, neutron or proton. ....

....

REFERENCES

[1] C. F. Weizsacker, Z. Phys. **96**, 431 (1935)

[2] A. Bohr and B. R. Mottelson, **Nuclear Structure**, Vol I (Benjamin, New York, 1969).

[3] H. A. Bethe and R. F. Bacher, Rev. Mod. Phys. **8**, 82 (1936).

[4] M. A. Preston and R. K. Bhaduri, **Structure of the Nucleus** (Addison Wesley, Reading, MA, 1975).

[5] A. W. Steiner, M. Prakash, J. M. Lattimer, and P. J. Ellis, Phys. Rep. **411**, 325 (2005).

[6] P. Danielewicz and J. Lee, Int. J. Mod. Phys. E**18**, 829 (2009) (Nucl. Phys. A**818**, 36 (2009)).

[7] S. J. Lee and A. Z. Mekjian, Phys. Rev. C**82**, 064319 (2010).

[8] S. J. Lee and A. Z. Mekjian, Phys. Rev. C**79**, 044323 (2009).

[9] S. J. Lee and A. Z. Mekjian, Phys. Rev. C**77**, 054612 (2008).

[10] S. J. Lee and A. Z. Mekjian, Phys. Lett. **580**, 137 (2004).

[11] S. J. Lee and A. Z. Mekjian, Phys. Rev. C**68**, 014608 (2003).

[12] W. D. Myers, W. J. Swiatecki, Nucl. Phys. A**81**, 1 (1966).

[13] W. D. Myers, W. J. Swiatecki, Ann. Phys. **55**, 395 (1969).

[14] W. D. Myers, W. J. Swiatecki, Ann. Phys. **84**, 186 (1974).

[15] W. D. Myers, **Droplet Model of Atomic Nuclei**, IFI/Plenum, New York, 1975.

Index

A/D converter, 50

Adams-Bashforth method, 14

Adams-Moulton method, 15

Bessel equation, 25

Bessel function, 26

Bode's rule, 10

boundary condition, 17, 39

- Dirichlet, 39
- Neumann, 40

C language, 6, 83

chi square fitting, 59

D/A converter, 49

damped gradient iteration, 34

determinant, 33

eigenfunction, 21

eigenvalue, 17, 21, 32

eigenvector, 32

elliptic differential equation, 37, 40, 44

error of measurement, 55

- random, 55
  - characteristics of, 56
- systematic, 55

Euler's method, 14

fast Fourier transform, 63

Fortran language, 5, 77

Gauss-Jordan method, 30

Gauss-Legendre quadrature, 28

Gaussian elimination method, 42

Gaussian quadrature, 27

Gram-Schmidt orthogonalization, 35

Green function, 20

Green's theorem, 20

HTML, 5, 71

hyperbolic differential equation, 38, 41

initial condition, 17
inverse vector iteration, 33
iterative Gauss-Seidel method, 40

Lagrange Interpolation, 7
Lanczos algorithm, 34
LaTeX, 66, 89
Legendre equation, 24
Legendre polynomial, 24, 28

matrix inversion, 30
mean value, 56, 59
metropolis algorithm, 47
Monte-Carlo simulation, 45

Neumann function, 26
Newton-Raphson method, 11
numerical differentiation, 8
numerical integral, 10, 27, 46
Numerov algorithm, 18, 19

orthogonality, 25, 62
  Legendre polynomial, 25, 28
  spherical harmonics, 25

parabolic differential equation, 37, 40
Predictor-Corrector algorithm, 15, 19

Runge-Kutta method, 15

Secant method, 11
shooting method, 21
Simpson's rule, 10
special function, 24, 62
spherical Bessel function, 27
standard deviation
  of data, 57
  of mean value, 57, 62

variational principle, 38

wavelet analysis, 64

다양한 컴퓨터 기능을 이용한

전산물리

2013년 12월 15일 인쇄
2013년 12월 20일 발행

저 자 ◎ 이 석 준
발 행 인 ◎ 조 승 식
발 행 처 ◎ (주)도서출판 북스힐
서울시 강북구 한천로 153길 17
등 록 ◎ 제 22-457 호

TEL (02) 994-0071(代)
FAX (02) 994-0073
E-MAIL bookswin@unitel.co.kr
www.bookshill.com

값 10,000원

잘못된 책은 교환해 드립니다.

ISBN 978-89-5526-552-1